# Deali
## with t
# EMPLOYEE
## FROM HEL

# Dealing
# with the
# EMPLOYEE
# FROM HELL

## A GUIDE TO COACHING
## AND MOTIVATION

### SHAUN BELDING

**KOGAN PAGE**

**Publisher's note**

Every possible effort has been made to ensure that the information contained in this book is accurate at the time of going to press, and the publishers and authors cannot accept responsibility for any errors or omissions, however caused. No responsibility for loss or damage occasioned to any person acting, or refraining from action, as a result of the material in this publication can be accepted by the editor, the publisher or any of the authors.

Previously published in Canada in 2004 by ECW Press, 2120 Queen Street East, Suite 200, Ontario, Canada M4E 1EZ entitled *Winning with the Employee from Hell*

First published in Great Britain in 2005 by Kogan Page Limited entitled *Dealing with the Employee from Hell*

Kogan Page Limited
120 Pentonville Road
London N1 9JN
United Kingdom
www.kogan-page.co.uk

**British Library Cataloguing in Publication Data**

A CIP record for this book is available from the British Library.

ISBN 0 7494 4453 3

Typeset by Saxon Graphics Ltd, Derby
Printed and bound in Great Britain by Creative Print and Design (Wales), Ebbw Vale

This book is dedicated to Mum, for all the lessons – especially the ones about looking for the good in other people. (I really was paying attention, you know.)

# Contents

# Introduction: into the depths of hell

*What's a little severance pay between friends?*

It's Tom. He's driving me mad. He's just so... well... negative. He always has that sarcastic comment, you know? As though he feels he has to judge everything. He's constantly taking shots at management, how bad all the decisions are and how stupid all the people around him are. It's just so hard to build any motivation or excitement about things because he makes people so cynical. I know it sounds like it's not a big deal – but I get a knot in my stomach every time I walk by him. I always wonder what he's saying about me when I'm not around...

Sound familiar? Tom is just one of those delightful employees who can make you question your decision to enter the field of management. Sometimes it seems that you no sooner get one Tom figured out than somebody else pops into your life with a whole new way to drive you mad. Employees from Hell – ambassadors for antacids everywhere.

They're not all like Tom, of course. Some are well meaning but lazy. Others are overly social. Some are downright criminal. The stories I've heard range from run-of-the-mill performance issues to toe-curling horror stories, from salaried sales reps sitting in the pub every day from noon until closing time to an employee who ran a phone sex line at work during working hours. They come in every shape and size, and they are all adept at increasing your stress levels.

I'm willing to bet that, if you've been in management for any time at all, you have either experienced or know someone who has experienced an Employee from Hell. I suppose it comes with the territory. What makes such employees so interesting is that they can get to you no matter how experienced you are. Whether you are a newcomer or have been in management for a hundred years, somebody somewhere is going to surprise you by doing something more stupid than the last person.

A good friend of mine, a general manager for a car rental company, once enthusiastically introduced me to the company's new training manager. I was instantly impressed: he was bright, enthusiastic, knowledgeable and personable. Some of the things he had already done for the company were, to say the least, spectacular. I remember thinking that he could have been a walking advert for the ideal training manager.

Eight months later, however, his employment at the company was terminated. On top of a fairly long list of wrongdoings during his brief tenure, it turns out that he was using the company's fleet to operate his own little private rental agency out the back door. To this day, my friend just shakes his head. This was a young man with the world at his feet. What on earth was he thinking?

Actually, that's a good question. What *are* these types of employees thinking? Are they even thinking at all? If we want to learn how to deal effectively with Employees from Hell, we first need to understand who they are and what makes them tick.

Who is the Employee from Hell? I suppose the simplest way to define him or her is as any employee with whom you are having an ongoing challenge. The challenge can involve any combination of work skills, interpersonal skills, attitude, aptitude, knowledge, intensity, personal situation or confidence. The Employee from Hell can be affecting you alone or any number of other people. Who are your Employees from Hell? They are the ones who continually come up in your conversations with your spouse, friends or peers. They are the ones you lose sleep over and the ones you dread having to see.

They are also often the roadblocks to achieving your goals, which is one of the reasons they create so much stress. Let's face it, for managers in today's business world, *productivity* is the measure of success. And anyone who, either consciously or unconsciously, stands in the way of that productivity also stands in the way of your happiness and future.

So why are they doing these things? What makes them tick? Is it just personality quirks? Are they just plain stupid? Is it intentional, or is it something else?

Unfortunately, and as sad as it sounds, some of the behaviour we see *is* intentional. Some people out there make deliberate efforts to work against you. Sometimes they just don't want to go in the direction you're pushing them. Sometimes they think that you are asking too much of them, and sometimes they believe that you're simply incompetent and therefore resent taking directions from you.

Fortunately, though, the majority of our challenges exist with people who are neither consciously nor deliberately trying to be a problem. They are, for the most part, either unaware of the impacts of their actions (or inactions) or simply unable to meet your expectations. They're just people, like you and me, with weaknesses, faults and frailties that are causing challenges. They aren't going out of their way to be difficult, but nevertheless the impact they can have on you can go far beyond your day-to-day interactions with them.

The owner of a wholesaling company once hired my company to help fix some serious morale challenges developing in one of his locations. Our first step was to meet with some of the people in the organization, and it didn't take many meetings to discover the root of the challenges.

Susan, the warm, bright and highly motivated manager, knew that there were issues but had no idea how to fix them. Her best friend, Carol, who had started as a colleague in the facility, wasn't responding well to Susan now being her new boss. She'd been there as long as Susan and thought that it was inappropriate for Susan to be giving her directions. In addition to a fairly consistent passive–aggressive response to Susan's leadership, Carol was continually searching for flaws and communicating her critical thoughts on Susan's management abilities to the other staff.

A couple of months into her tenure as manager, Susan made the mistake of bringing her husband, a handyman, in to do a bit of much-needed work. Carol made a point of identifying all of the errors in his work and then lamenting to everyone how, because it was Susan's husband, it was now impossible to bring it to her attention without offending her.

By the time we got involved, Susan could barely bring herself even to look at Carol, much less talk to her. And it seemed to Susan that every initiative she tried to introduce was now being met with resistance from everyone.

Was Carol deliberately trying to hurt Susan and her company? I don't think so. Carol was operating on instinct and emotion without being aware of either the motivations for her actions or the consequences she had created. Unfortunately, the effect of a little jealousy in a 'friend' and colleague had gone far beyond just the two of them. Productivity in the warehouse had decreased by almost 20 per cent, and employee turnover had sharply increased. The impacts on Susan's personal life were equally profound. Her relationship with her husband had become strained, and her normally positive and cheerful disposition had become negative and irritable.

As with all difficult people, Employees from Hell stand out in our minds and occupy our thoughts so much because they are exceptions, not the norm. But even though they may not come around that often, they can still create long-lasting havoc for a business and the collective psyche of your team. Your ability to manage these people in an effective and proactive manner is crucial to everyone involved. And the consequences of mismanaging them or, worse, not managing them can be disastrous.

Employees from Hell can be divided into two distinct groups: Performance Challenges and Personality Challenges, and I separate the two in this book because they are quite different in how they need to be approached. Performance Challenges, as the name suggests, are employees whom you are having difficulty bringing up to standard. They are either unable or unwilling to perform to a level that you consider acceptable. Personality Challenges are employees who, while competent, are disruptive because of their attitudes or interpersonal skills. While many of them get their jobs done, they have detrimental effects on the team and the environment.

There is, of course, one strategy that works for people in both groups: you could just fire them. After all, what's a little severance pay between friends? Assuming you are fortunate enough to hire better the next time, your problem is solved – cleanly and simply. The quandary with this strategy is that you risk throwing out the wheat with the proverbial chaff. Not all Employees from Hell, after all, are a complete liability to the company. Their current actions might be a challenge, but the employees themselves might have the potential to be tremendously valuable. They might possess knowledge or skills that are either an asset to the business or hard to find in a new recruit. They might be contributing in other areas of the business. They might be worth trying to save.

It's also a good idea, before you fire someone, to take into account the role that you may have played in that person's behaviour. The person you consider to be an Employee from Hell may be a model employee to another manager. Early in my career, I inherited a secretary whom my predecessor, a long-time acquaintance, claimed he was going to steal back from me as soon as he had the chance. 'She's amazing', I remember him telling me. 'I've never worked with a more efficient person. It's as though she can read my mind.' He eventually did steal her from me, but it wasn't soon enough for my liking. I found her cold, humourless and unwilling to make any extra effort.

I discovered several years later that my friend had always made a point of including her in all his meetings, regardless of whom they were with, so that she'd always been completely up to speed on his activities and upcoming workloads. She had really appreciated it, and it had given her a sense of importance in the organization. I hadn't thought to do this, and she'd taken the absence of invitations to my meetings as my way of saying 'Just do your own job, and never mind mine.' The challenge, as it turned out, wasn't as much my employee as my own lack of communication and leadership skills. As Ralph Waldo Emerson once wrote, 'To different minds, the same world is a hell, and a heaven.'

In this book, I will introduce specific and powerful management strategies that are worth exploring before resorting to that unenjoyable end game of dismissing employees. The book begins with some proactive management practices for creating an environment that minimizes the potential for employee discontent. It includes skills and processes that are remarkably effective in dealing with Performance Challenges. And it outlines successful techniques for managing a wide variety of common Personality Challenges.

Perhaps more importantly, in *Dealing with the Employee from Hell* I try to explain why some people behave in such seemingly inexplicable ways. We will also look at why some of the traditional, popular management strategies don't work consistently and why some don't really work at all. Fundamentally, this book is about people – what makes them tick and how to work with them.

I'm afraid that, if you're looking for some new buzzwords with which to impress your friends, you may be disappointed. *The purpose of this book is to provide straightforward, real-life solutions to real-life challenges faced every day by people who manage people.* All of those important-sounding words and phrases – client-centric, human capital, core competencies, gap analyses, best practices, learning metrics and so on – may look great in a vision paper or strategic document, but I have always found them to be counterproductive when it actually comes to getting things done. Far too few people have a real under-standing of what they look like in real-life situations. This is a plain and straightforward book, and the measure of its success will be simple: if you can inspire just one difficult employee to become a motivated, loyal and productive member of your team, then we've all won – you, me, your employee and your company.

# 1

# What employees want

*It's not so much knowing what to do as it is doing what you know.*

Ah, the good old days. Let your employees in, lock the door, chain them to their desks and don't let them out until the job is done. You want to motivate them? Start yelling and badgering, and threaten not to pay them unless they smarten up. Yes, life certainly was good back then. If only it could still be so simple.

Now we have to contend with sick leave, maternity leave, stress leave, counsellors and coaches, daycare centres, hiring bonuses, extended holidays, sensitivity training, flexitime and a myriad of special perks and incentives. Long gone are the days when MBA (management by abuse) style leadership was accepted by all.

Hard to understand, really. After all, there are 168 hours in a week. If you factor in eight hours a day for sleep, two hours for breakfasts, dinners, showers, toilet breaks and so on, and another hour per day for commuting, you're left with about 93 available hours per week. If you have a nine-to-five job (OK, as though anyone's got one of those any more), that means spending only 43 per cent of your available hours at work. Recent studies actually suggest that the real number is more than 50 per cent, but it still means that average people have about half of their waking hours to themselves. What more do they want?

A lot more, it seems. Quite a lot more. The HR people I talk to, for example, tell me that workplace environment, holidays and other benefits are inexorably creeping up on salary as primary markers of employee satisfaction. That age-old question – do you live to work or work to live? – is seeping back into our social consciousness. People want working to be, as much as possible, an enjoyable experience. And if you can't provide that for them, either they're going to leave for someone who can or they're going to start moaning so much that your life will become a living hell. Neither is a pleasant option.

Employees from Hell, for the most part, aren't just crazy people that you had the misfortune to hire at a weak moment. Nor are most of them just naturally disgruntled people. History has repeatedly shown that, as an environment changes, so do the people in it. Put a typically good person in a bad environment, and that person's behaviour will begin to deteriorate. Put a typically bad person in a good environment, and that person's behaviour will begin to improve. My experience has been that most people in this world are pretty decent. Of course, some are a little louder, some are a little more aggressive and some are a little stranger, but most people seem to make an effort to get along. We just have to make sure that we have the right conditions to facilitate playing nicely together.

So, before we begin to examine the employees, let's take a look at what's going on around them that could be contributing to their unproductive or counterproductive behaviour. It's an important exercise. We want to make sure that we'll be solving a problem instead of just masking symptoms. Like a doctor doing a diagnosis of a patient with a sore throat, you first want to find out what's causing the problem. A throat lozenge may ease the pain temporarily, but, if the root of the problem is something more serious, antibiotics or some other form of treatment may be required. As in medicine, so in a business environment, failure to address the direct cause can have serious and unpleasant repercussions.

To determine if an employee's negative behaviour stems from his or her own personal quirks, or is a symptom of something more systemic, you have to examine a few things. You have to look at the environment. You have to look at yourself as a manager. You have to look at the employee's expectations of you and the company, how reasonable those expectations are and the degree to which they are being met. Why did the employee choose to work for your company in the first place? What roles does the employee expect you and your company to play in the employee–employer contract? You may have some pretty clear expectations of what you want from the employee, but what does the employee expect from you?

Let's begin by examining why your employees chose to work for your company in the first place. People choose a place of work for many different reasons: salary and benefits, proximity to home, the types of products and services the company is involved in, the employee's area of expertise, and the working environment, to name just a few. In many cases, your company became the company of choice simply because you were the first to hire them.

These criteria play a large role in employee expectations. An employee who gets a sizeable rise still may not be happy if the job isn't challenging or within the employee's area of expertise. A change in location can be a hardship for someone used to walking to work. An additional week's holiday instead of a rise may mean nothing to the employee facing tuition fees for a child's university education. A shift to lower-profile projects can be perceived as thwarting an employee's opportunities for advancement.

The managing director of a car servicing company once told me of the time he tried to lighten the load of an overworked director by transferring some of the director's responsibilities to another department. As it turned out, his attempt to do something positive for a valued employee backfired. The director became distraught, thinking that the move was a reflection of the MD's confidence in him, and almost quit the company.

The expectations that employees have of your company will vary based on the nature of their work and their positions within the company. A senior executive, for example, probably expects an office with a window, a nice desk, a comfortable chair, guest chairs, a coffee-table, etc. A miner working a mile below the surface, on the other hand, has quite different expectations. He might expect ready availability of emergency oxygen, up-to-date equipment and cold water. The senior manager expects from the boss latitude to make decisions and take action. The miner expects clear direction and a fair workload.

## DARTs

Are there any expectations common to all employees? Are there any general guidelines we can use to ensure that we are at least on the right track, no matter what business we are in, who our employees are and what type of work they do? Yes, there are. They are simple and seemingly straightforward, and will probably resonate with you immediately because they are the same expectations you have of the people to whom you report. Without exception, whenever my company is asked to help re-energize a faltering workplace environment, the people we interview cite them instantly as the missing elements of their happiness: direction, appreciation, respect and tools (DARTs, if you happen to enjoy acronyms).

Direction, appreciation, respect and tools. These are the absolute basics of people management, and they are taught in different fashions in virtually every management skills seminar out there. Yet a colossal number of employees believe that those elements are lacking in their working environments. Why is this happening?

Before we take a look at why, let's do a quick review of these four elements and why they are important.

## Direction

Think about the young child who walks on to the field to take part in a game of football. The first question to come out of the child's mouth is always the same: 'Which team am I on?' The child, like us, wants to know which way to run, whom to pass the ball to and which net to aim at. The clearer and more accurate the directions that we as managers give to our employees, the better the results and the happier everyone is.

## Appreciation

Many years ago, I worked in the advertising agency business. One of my clients was a large trust company gearing up for the lucrative retirement savings programme season. We were under the gun (as always seemed to be the case in that industry), and as manager of the project I had to work right through the Christmas season. Twelve hours a day, including Christmas Eve, Boxing Day, New Year's Eve and New Year's Day. For three straight weeks, the only day I got off was Christmas. The director I reported to, holidaying in the Caribbean for those three weeks, returned, and the first thing he did was tear a strip off me because the project wasn't further along. There was no recognition whatsoever of the work and commitment I'd put into the project. It was at that moment I decided to leave the company. It's very easy to forget how powerful a simple thank-you can be. We all like to be recognized for our efforts.

## Respect

In addition to the effort we put in, we like to be recognized for our abilities and treated with the same kind of dignity we give to those around us. In our society, we consider dignity to be a fundamental right – regardless of rank, position or power. In my experience, most employees have no problem with managers who are exacting, as long as they are not disrespectful. There is never a pay-off for managers in ignoring common courtesy.

## Tools

A couple of Christmases ago, my wife bought me a cordless drill. I can't get over the huge difference it has made in completing all the little projects she has me do. (Now that I think of it, there might have been an ulterior motive for the gift.) No more digging out an extension cord, unwinding it, plugging it in, rewinding it, putting it away – just pick up the drill, do the job and put the drill away. It has increased my household project productivity tremendously.

The same scenario holds true in the workplace. Just as you wouldn't hire carpenters and not give them hammers, you wouldn't hire assistants and not give them computers or sales-people and not give them professional presentation material. Intellectual tools are no different from physical tools in this regard. Whenever my company conducts a seminar, workshop or clinic, there is at least one person who says to us 'I wish I had known some of this stuff years ago.' We love to hear that. Because that is precisely why the company hired us in the first place – to give its employees some intellectual tools to help them do their jobs better.

These four elements, DARTs, are the backbone of successful team leadership, and they represent the minimum that your employees expect from you. They seem to be common sense, and most experienced managers consider them the basics. But if DARTs are in fact such common sense, why do so many people perceive them to be lacking in their work environments?

There are two reasons. The first and simplest reason is that, as in any other occupation, in management people range from being very good to very bad. The bad managers either don't know or don't care about the importance of direction, appreci-ation, respect and tools. The second and, I believe, more common reason has more to do with perception and perspective than skill or attitude. I've encountered many managers who understand the fundamentals of team leadership and (although their employees will tell quite different stories) believe that they are making solid attempts to use these skills. They think they are doing these things, but they're not. It goes back to that ancient adage: 'It's not so much knowing what to do as it is doing what you know.'

I will never forget one afternoon I spent coaching in a unisex clothing shop. I was working with one of the employees on her discovery skills and encouraging her to ask more probing questions of her customers. Julie made remarkable progress as the day went on. Two hours into the session, she completed a £400 sale from a customer who'd begun the interaction with 'No thanks, I'm just looking.' On the way out the door, the customer remarked to her 'You're wonderful! I'm going to send all my friends in to see you.' Julie was on top of the world. Her excitement and confidence were palpable as she went from customer to customer. I took this opportunity to step out for a bite of lunch.

Forty-five minutes later, I walked back into the shop only to find Julie standing behind the counter with a long face and the customers in the shop being virtually ignored. It was a shocking contrast to the woman I'd seen less than an hour before. 'What's going on?' I asked. 'When I left, you were bouncing off the ceiling. Now you look like the world is coming to an end. Is everything all right?'

Julie looked at me for a moment and then said glumly 'Yes, my manager came in shortly after you left. I told him about the big sale I made and all the questions I asked.' Her voice started to become excited again as she continued. 'And I told him about how she was originally just looking and how I managed to make her feel comfortable with me. And I told him about how she thought I was wonderful and that she was going to send all of her friends to the shop.' At this point, her voice faltered, and she said 'And my manager just looked at me and said "So are you just going to stand around and brag about it all day, or are you going to get back to work?"'

It still ranks in the top five stupid things I've ever heard of a manager saying. It also surprised me. I had spent some time with Craig, the manager, the day before, and he had struck me as a bright, positive and motivated young man. The comment seemed to be completely out of character. When I saw him an hour later, I asked him about it.

Craig was mortified when I told him of the effect of his comment on Julie. 'It was a totally tongue-in-cheek response', he said to me earnestly. 'I was thrilled with what she had done. As a matter of fact, I got straight on the phone to our district manager to tell her about it. Here, look what just came in.' He handed me a fax for Julie from the district manager that had come in five minutes earlier congratulating her on the sale. What Craig had really meant was 'I'm proud of you – now go out and do it again!' Unfortunately, Julie hadn't realized this and had taken his comment literally. Craig learnt a valuable lesson on perspective that day.

## The telescope effect

There is a fascinating product of employer–employee perspective that I refer to as 'the telescope effect'. Imagine holding a telescope as you normally would and looking through the eyepiece. The object you are focused on zooms closer until you almost think you can reach out and touch it. It's right there. Now turn the telescope around and look at the same object through the other end. The object now appears tiny and a great distance away.

The same phenomenon, interestingly, also exists between employees and bosses. Most progressive managers these days refer to their employees as 'the team' and talk about them as 'working with me' instead of 'working for me'. Most managers perceive the gap between themselves and their employees as being relatively small. They are looking through the eyepiece of the telescope. They consider themselves part of the team and, although in a management position, not necessarily superior to those around them. In theory, it's a great attitude and is common to most strong leaders. It can work against you, however, when you fail to recognize that employees see the distance as significantly greater.

How do you perceive your own boss? Do you feel as close in position to your boss as you do to your employees? There is a good chance you don't. And, when you think about it, it makes sense. Your boss is the one who evaluates your work and judges your performance. Your boss is the one who determines what you do and has to make sure you do it. To varying degrees, your boss determines your salary and your opportunities for advancement. Your boss is the controlling factor in 50 per cent of your available waking hours. No matter how nice your boss may be, or how team focused his or her approach may be, you will always perceive the gap between the two of you to be much greater than the boss will. With your boss, you're looking through the other end of the telescope.

What is the impact of this telescope effect on the employer–employee relationship? The primary impact has to do with weight and gravity. It's a physics thing. Think of any statement you make as being a brick, and your position power as the distance above the person to whom you make the statement. Whenever you speak, then, it's like dropping that brick on the person's head.

Now imagine saying jokingly to a good friend 'You are so lazy!' What would the impact be? It would, of course, be minimal. Because you occupy no position power over your friend, you are both at the same height. The effect would be the same as simply placing the brick on your friend's head.

Imagine, however, making the same statement to an employee. Because you don't perceive a great deal of position power, you might assume a similar impact. But because your employee perceives your position power as being much greater, to the employee the impact is the same as if you dropped the brick from many feet up. 'Was the boss really joking?' the employee might think. 'Was the boss trying to make a point?' 'I wonder if the boss really thinks I'm lazy.' 'What if the boss was being serious?' The employee would feel significant pain that you didn't even realize you had delivered.

The stronger the statement, and the higher your position, the bigger the brick is, and the faster and harder it drops. The CEO who visits one of the plant's assembly lines and comments to an employee that his or her work is substandard therefore delivers a devastating blow.

We always have to be aware of our employees' perspectives. What you consider to be adequate direction, appreciation, respect and tools may not appear so to your employees. Julie didn't recognize Craig's flippant comment as appreciation. My secretary viewed not being invited to meetings as a lack of respect. An employee given a lot of latitude in a project could conceivably perceive it as a lack of direction.

Delivering those things that make for an enjoyable work environment also means having tremendous awareness of the people around you. This is particularly true during times of stress and high workload. Sometimes when we become so engrossed in our own challenges, we forget to do the simple things we know we should be doing. We speak more sharply to people than is appropriate. We forget that it's been six months and we still haven't given our employees that training they need to do the job better. We stop doing what we know.

As with most difficult situations, those involving Employees from Hell are often born of the discrepancy between expectations and reality. The better we understand those expectations, particularly as they relate to direction, appreciation, respect and tools, and the closer we get to meeting them, the less of a breeding ground there is for future challenges.

# 2

# Setting the stage

*Pardac is a good thing.*

'I don't get ulcers – I'm a carrier' is the favourite quip of a senior executive I know. It isn't really true in his case, but it is, unfortunately, an all-too-real scenario in the working world. It's amazing how many 'difficult employee' situations actually turn out to be manager behaviours and company policies that have set things up for failure. Often it's not the employee that is the real problem. Let's face it, if you poke a dog long enough with a stick, you're going to get bitten – even by the friendly ones.

Some company policies and management behaviours are almost guaranteed to create discontented and disruptive employees, and it's important that we take a look at them. Before we begin to point fingers at our employees, we want to make sure that we're not at the root of the problem. Following is a checklist of what I've found to be the seven most important things a company should do to minimize employee challenges.

## 1. Become a better boss

It's amazing how, as our skill levels increase, our challenges with employees decrease. Read books (and the next chapter); go to seminars; get a personal coach. Make every effort you can to ensure that you're doing the best job possible. Make your efforts visible to people. Let them know what you're doing. Ask them for their insights, opinions and guidance. Part of a boss's job is to be a role model for employees. And that means walking the proverbial talk. If you're asking your staff to improve performance or behaviour, you have to let them know that the same expectations apply to everyone – even you.

Part of this process also means learning how to ask yourself slightly different questions than you're used to – questions that are a bit more introspective. For example, instead of asking yourself 'Why does the employee do that?' you could ask yourself 'What am I doing that is causing the employee to do that?' It might turn out that an employee's unsatisfactory behaviour has nothing to do with something you've done, but, if you don't ask yourself the question, you'll never know.

Like it or not, employees are reflections of their managers. Walk into an office environment and see a group of serious and sullen people working at their desks; then meet the manager, and guess what you'll find – a serious and sullen manager. Walk into a shop and find unhelpful, grumpy staff who don't seem to have any clue what customer service is all about, and guess what you'll find? You've got it – a manager who sends the same message. The reverse is also true. Walk into a business environment and find an energized and positive group of people, and you'll find an energized and positive manager.

One of the most amazing work environments I've ever seen was at a company called Zenastra Photonics. The very air was alive with energy and charged with excitement. The sense of team spirit and camaraderie was unlike anything I'd witnessed before. Small wonder. The CEO and CFO used to make regular tours of the company – talking, joking, laughing and interacting with people. Zenastra unfortunately fell victim to the high-tech meltdown of the late 1990s, but it certainly wasn't because of poor management. To this day, former Zenastra employees get together for parties and networking sessions. According to Doug Gibson, the CFO, there were 250 employees and not an Employee from Hell among them. What a coincidence.

# 2. Create an enjoyable environment

It is not difficult to create an enjoyable environment for your staff. Creating a positive and enjoyable environment is largely about the little things. If you're in an office environment, make sure everyone has a comfortable chair. Get employees incandescent lights for their desks to counter the draining-effect of fluorescent lighting. Pin up a joke-of-the-day cartoon on your office door (doing this also has the pleasant side-effect of making people more comfortable coming to your office). Have a games day once a month, perhaps playing interoffice minigolf in the corridors. A CEO I know set up an annual tricycle race on a track created in the company's corridors.

One of my company's call centre clients once developed a tremendous incentive game to encourage employees to deal with problem situations themselves instead of escalating them to more senior levels. The company created a Customer from Hell dartboard. Every time employees got a difficult customer and handled the situation themselves, they got a dart to throw at the board. Marked on the different segments of the board were various prizes, ranging from a £5 gift token for the local coffee shop to dinner for two at a local restaurant. Every time someone handled a difficult situation, that person would hang up the phone and shout for a dart. Everyone would then turn to see what the person won. Not only did the game bring a little more fun into the work environment, but it was also tremendously successful in reducing the number of escalated calls.

If you want to improve your work environment, the best way to start is by asking people what they think would make an improvement. Begin by talking to everyone on your team. Don't send out a memo or an impersonal blanket e-mail – make it a personal visit. Tell your team you'd like their feedback on how to make the work environment more pleasant. Give them sheets of paper to write their ideas on, and have them drop the sheets in a box outside your office by the end of the day. Allow them to make their suggestions anonymously, just in case somebody wants to tell you something you don't really want to hear.

Be careful when introducing incentive games, however. Some people, for example, respond well to competition, while others respond better to cooperative incentives. To make these games work, you need a good understanding of your team and where each member is coming from. Chapter 9, on external motivation, should give you a good start on this understanding.

## 3. Communicate with your employees

A huge proportion of interoffice challenges stems from communication breakdowns. As a manager, you have to maximize both the frequency and the quality of your communications. Sometimes the most insidious and destructive forces affecting an office environment are rumours and office gossip. Both are fuelled by lack of communication and incomplete information. One person has a titbit of information (or misinformation) that someone else wants to hear, and that person passes it on to the next person, and so on, with the story changing slightly every time. Just like that game we used to play in primary school. The best way to counteract this problem is to make sure that people don't feel uninformed. The more you can tell employees, the better.

Garry Wood, when he took over as president and CEO of Bell Distribution Inc in the United States, introduced to the company the concept of monthly 'Power Sessions'. They are one- to two-hour updates held at the head office on every aspect of the business. Attendance isn't mandatory, but all BDI employees are invited, and the atmosphere is charged with electricity. Beginning with Garry, different people get up and deliver brief, punchy messages to the large audience. The previous month's and year-to-date successes are celebrated, and areas for improvement are acknowledged. Promotions and contests are introduced. Individuals are recognized for notable accomplishments. The last half-hour is a question-and-answer session in which any employee is free to ask any question of the senior management team.

The sense of pride and accomplishment within BDI is palpable. Not only are all employees conscious of the company's direction, but they are also aware of the challenges the company is facing and how it is handling them. BDI gets the message out, and the result is a highly motivated and satisfied workforce.

The way messages are sent also plays a role in effective communication. E-mail, the replacement for the interoffice memo, has become one of the most misused forms of communication in the new millennium. I've heard literally hundreds of stories of employees receiving e-mail memos from bosses sitting in offices just a few feet away from them. The fact is, there is simply no better way to communicate with someone than to talk face to face. Of course, sometimes doing so takes a little longer. Sometimes it takes a lot longer. But the impact on both productivity and employee satisfaction makes it more than just a little worthwhile. One very effective director whom I know proudly claims that every e-mail he sends out to his staff begins with 'As you already know…'. That is because, before he sends the confirming e-mail, he has already discussed the matter with each member of his team.

Communication, of course, goes both ways. Not only do you have to enhance the way you communicate with your employees, but you also have to create an environment in which they can easily communicate with you. Keep in mind the telescope effect, and remember that your employees are less comfortable initiating communications with you than you are with them.

Begin with an open-door policy. A real open-door policy. Be careful you don't have one of those 'My-door-is-always-open-but-if-you-walk-through-it-I'm-going-to-be-annoyed' policies, as so many managers tend to have. Your employees – all of them – must feel completely comfortable approaching you about any topic. But how can you achieve this level of comfort? How can you convince your employees, some of whom may be tremendously intimidated by either you or your position, that you are, in fact, approachable? The best method is the tried-and-true MBWA: management by walking around.

The best boss I ever had was Don Ambrose, chairman of the advertising agency Ambrose, Carr, Deforest & Linton. He was a master of MBWA. Everyone in the agency knew that between 7.30 and 8.00 every morning Don made the rounds of the office. If you had a pressing issue that you wanted to talk to him about, you simply had to be in your office when he walked by. Sometimes he'd just poke his head inside your office to say hello, and sometimes he'd sit down and have a little chat. But if you had something on your mind, he was always open to listening to it. He didn't wait for people to open his door. He opened their doors. The net result of this approach was twofold. First, Don was by far the most informed person in the office. Second, there were rarely any issues left to fester.

Even if you don't have a door to open, you can still get the quality of feedback you want. A regional manager for a retail chain once shared with me her secret for getting open and honest feedback from shop employees. Prior to every shop staff meeting she attended, she would give them pieces of paper and ask them to write down suggestions for improving something within the shop, frustrations or problems, or something or someone worthy of praise. They were not to put their names on the papers. At the staff meeting, they would fold their pieces of paper and deposit them in a large box. She would shake the box to mix up the papers, then have everyone draw out one of them. Each person would then read out in turn what was on his or her sheet of paper, and the team would have a discussion about the point that had been made.

The beauty of this method was that little things were brought out and discussed in a public forum before they became serious issues. And employees could raise these issues without fear of repercussion. The key to this process, claimed the regional manager, is that, whenever an issue was brought up, even if it was about her or the managers, nobody was allowed to become defensive. Points of view were acknowledged and respected, and debate was encouraged. After four or five of those meetings, she claimed, the box became virtually unnecessary since employees began to trust that they could express themselves without repercussions during normal working hours.

The biggest challenge in improving communication is that most of us already consider ourselves pretty good communicators. We tend to perceive communication challenges as originating with somebody else, not us. In fact, most of us are mediocre communicators at best. In my company's leadership and team-building workshops and retreats, we always include one or two communication exercises so that people can test their own communication skills. Participants are always surprised at how little of what they say actually gets across to the recipient and how little of what the other person says they actually absorb.

# 4. Lose the stupid rules

I will never forget sitting in a newspaper reporter's office and reading through an 'office rules reminder' memo. Among other things, it included:

- no mobile phone use in the office;
- no dating company employees;
- no cartoons on the wall; and
- no running in the corridor.

I laughed, assuming that it was a tongue-in-cheek missive, and then was astounded to learn that it was serious indeed. 'We're surrounded by PC Nazis and office police', he lamented. 'If I didn't work outside of the office so much, I would have quit long ago.'

While most of the rules astonished me, I was particularly curious about the one banning 'running in the corridor'. It turned out that a reporter had once been frantically dashing back to his office when he'd run squarely into the managing editor – sending his coffee flying. The angry editor had gone straight back to his office and issued the directive.

It was typical of the root cause of many stupid rules. Frustrated managers create blanket rules to solve specific problems. Instead of just dealing with individual behaviour, they pass laws that affect everyone. Remember the school-teacher who used to scold or punish the whole class when one person did something wrong? We all hated it then, and we all hate it now. As a manager, if you have a problem situation, deal with it. An official rule should always be a last resort.

All too often, managers are guilty of trying to control their environments through rules instead of respect. And, while it's good to have a professional conduct policy (reviewed by a lawyer), it's always better when people do things because they want to instead of because they have to. As we'll discuss in Chapter 4, having solid, positive and motivating performance standards is a far better tool for guiding employee performance than blanket rules.

Some rules are just plain silly. Edicts such as 'No dating other employees or customers' are virtually unenforceable. 'No personal plants' reduces employees' ability to make their environments more comfortable. The son of a good friend of mine, working in a fast-food restaurant, was once instructed to have his hair cut. It was no longer than the hair of the women who worked there, and he wore it in a hair net just as the women did, but there was a rule that men had to have short hair. Unfair and seemingly arbitrary rules such as that one just beg for conflict.

It's always a good idea to ask your employees to do a comprehensive critique of the office rules. You'll learn in a hurry which ones people aren't responding to well.

# 5. Use the power of pardac

'Employee empowerment' might well be the most overused buzzword yet poorly understood concept in today's business world. Its meaning is really quite simple: give your employees the tools and the authority to make decisions.

I remember being in a small city airport. A distraught young woman in front of us in the queue was desperately trying to get a ticket for the next flight, which was sold out. Her daughter was in hospital, gravely ill, and there were no other family members with her. The man behind the counter looked at her for a few moments, as if to size her up, and then looked back at his computer screen. When he looked up again, he said 'Don't you worry, madam, you're on the flight. Seat 14B. We'll get you there.'

When it was our turn at the counter, I asked him how he was able to get her on the flight. 'Well,' he said with a smile, 'the last person we check in is going to discover that we're overbooked. Somebody who's not in so much of a hurry is going to have to miss the flight. We'll give them some compensation for their inconvenience, and everybody will be happy.'

'That's good', I said, recalling my own experience trying to get a flight when my father passed away. 'I seem to remember going through a lot of paperwork and hassle to get the airline to make an exception like that.'

The man looked at me and smiled again. 'Well, at this little airport, we have pardac. Let me tell you something – it saves a lot of time and aggravation for everybody.'

Pardac, indeed? When we got on the plane, I turned to my business partner and asked him if he knew what 'pardac' was. He chuckled and pointed out that I had simply misunderstood the man's pronunciation and that he had really said 'power to act'. Here was a man given wide latitude to make decisions. The net result – less stress for him, less paperwork for his company, and happier customers. Of course, he probably made a poor decision occasionally, but the overall benefits far outweighed the risks.

Many companies don't empower their employees as much as they should because empowerment equals risk. There will always be people who make poor decisions, and there will always be people who take advantage of their expanded powers. What we so often lose sight of, however, is that for the most part these are the exceptions, not the rules. Assuming that you've hired well, that you've trained well and that you yourself have been a good role model, what is the real risk?

The risk, of course, is that employees might make mistakes that will cost you money in the short term. But, if you coach them properly and advise them of their errors, hopefully they won't repeat the mistakes. The question you should be asking, though, is what is the risk you run by not empowering your employees?

First, you risk increasing your own workload. Second, you risk slowing down processes, and that will cost the company money. Third, you risk making your employees feel less ownership over the actions they do take. And fourth, diminished control over their own destinies will create significant and ongoing frustration.

Pardac is a good thing.

# 6. Don't embarrass your employees

I remember walking through the doors of a well-known ice-cream franchise, and there, behind the counter, was the shop manager loudly and angrily berating one of his employees. Including me, there were four customers in the shop. The scene lasted a full three minutes. From what I could glean, the employee had forgotten to change some of the tubs in the freezer. Two of the customers were looking at each other in astonishment, and the third walked out. When it was my turn at the counter, I had a brief conversation with the manager, who had taken over from the now distraught employee. When no one was within earshot, I suggested to him that he consider not scolding his employees in front of customers. He looked at me unapologetically and said 'It wouldn't happen if she would just do her job right.' Not only had he embarrassed her in front of their customers, but he had also unwittingly embarrassed himself.

As we discussed in the first chapter when talking about DARTs, respect is one of the cornerstones of good management.

Respect is also reciprocal. Treat people with respect, and they will treat you with respect. Treat them disrespectfully, and expect the same in return. I have never seen a positive pay-off to embarrassing an employee in public.

# 7. Listen to your employees

In my first book, *Dealing with the Customer from Hell*, I described a six-step process for dealing with the majority of dissatisfied customers whom employees encounter. The process, using the acronym LESTER, demonstrates the tremendous power of active listening – a skill that is equally powerful in maintaining positive relationships with your employees.

'I keep telling the boss that this is what we should be doing, but the boss just doesn't listen!' is a statement I'm sure I've heard a thousand times from employees who are frustrated with their bosses. They feel neglected, underappreciated and unimportant – and the boss wonders why there is a morale challenge. Even if you do believe that you listen well, it is important to remember that listening by itself isn't good enough. You have to listen in such a way that people actually know you are listening. Here are some basic rules.

## Pay attention

When an employee has something to say, turn to the employee. Face the employee. Put down the thing you're working on and give the employee your undivided attention. Look into the employee's eyes, and let him or her know that, for the moment, he or she is the most important person in your universe.

## Find out the employee's thoughts

Usually, by the time your employee has brought something to your attention, he or she has already been thinking about it for a while. It's always a good idea to find out what's on the employee's mind. If it is something that requires action, find out what the employee thinks that action should be.

## Echo the employee's thoughts

After your employee has finished speaking, simply reflect the essence of the statement. If the employee is telling you that a new project is putting excessive pressure on the team, for example, simply say 'So you think this project is starting to get to people?' The employee gets the message that you've heard him or her. You might not agree with the employee, but you've heard him or her.

## Acknowledge the employee's ideas

If your employee has presented an idea to you, make a point of acknowledging it and the thought behind it. Often we are guilty of just grunting or nodding at an idea or, worse, trying to find flaws in it. A simple 'That's an interesting idea – thanks for bringing it up' is all you need.

## Set expectations

If your employee has presented you with an idea or thought that you may not be acting on for some time (if at all), make sure that the employee knows it. People are far more willing to accept delays when they are already expecting them. Say something like 'I can't promise that I'll jump on this right away – I'm really under the gun right now – but I will look into it over the next few months', and you will put people's minds at ease.

## Respond

You can't take an idea or suggestion from someone and then hope that over time the person will just forget about it. That's not going to happen. You are far better off saying something like 'I just wanted you to know that I've given your idea a lot of thought over the past couple of weeks, and I don't think we're going to be using it right now. Don't let that stop you from coming up with new ones, however – I really appreciate them!'

The active listening process opens up lines of communication and shuts down lines of miscommunication. There is no better way to maximize employee morale.

Here again are the key things to remember in setting the stage for an enjoyable workplace:

- Become a better boss.
- Create an enjoyable environment.
- Communicate with your employees.
- Lose the stupid rules.
- Empower your employees.
- Don't embarrass your employees.
- Listen to your employees.

# 3

# Anatomy of a great boss

*You get what you give.*

My business partner, Bob Hough, often talks about his former boss and long-time mentor, Hugh Burgess – now at Pitney Bowes. When I finally got to meet Hugh, I could understand why he had made such a positive impression on Bob. He exudes leadership with a laid-back attitude that makes people feel instantly comfortable with him.

According to Bob, their first encounter occurred when Hugh took over as corporate manager of the company Bob was working for. One of Hugh's initial acts was to call Bob and all of the other managers in for a meeting. The first words out of his mouth were 'You don't work for me.' A moment of panic hit Bob and the others as they thought they were being fired. They quickly realized otherwise. 'I work for you', continued Hugh. 'Your job is to make sure that the things get done that have to get done. My job is to make sure that you have everything you need to do your job well.' It is without question the most accurate and concise definition of a manager's role that I have ever heard. And I have probably repeated it a thousand times (always giving Hugh credit, of course).

When Bob first introduced me to Hugh, he casually dropped another piece of magnificent wisdom into my lap. We were in the middle of a lively discussion on management practices when Hugh laughed and said 'We can talk management theory all we want, but the most valuable piece of advice I've ever received was from my mother when I was just a kid: "You get what you give."'

In addition to all of his skills and knowledge, the thing that makes Hugh such a tremendous leader and manager is his clear understanding of a boss's role. He also understands the principle that, like it or not, the way our employees behave is a direct reflection of the way we manage them. You get what you give.

In the previous chapter, we talked about what our employees expect of us and our companies and what kinds of environments are least likely to create Employees from Hell. In this chapter, we're going to explore the impact that strong leadership has on employee behaviour and on the direct relationship between the strength of your leadership and the challenges you have with employees.

If you've ever gardened, or tried to create and maintain that perfect lawn, you will know intimately the powerful truth of the old adage 'an ounce of prevention is worth a pound of cure'. Putting a proper treatment on your lawn in the autumn and spring will save you countless hours of pulling out dandelions and other weeds. Any gardener or farmer will tell you that the better condition the soil is in when you begin, the less work you end up doing in the long run.

The same is true with people. Some bosses seemingly spend all their time pulling the weeds out of their companies – firing the people who aren't doing their jobs or don't fit in, only to have more challenges sprout up after they are gone. The companies and managers who are always the most successful, however, have created conditions so that those weeds don't grow in the first place. It all boils down to leadership.

# What leadership is all about

From the hundreds of excellent people out there who speak and write about leadership, the best definition of a leader that I have been able to piece together is 'a trusted and respected action taker focused on a common goal'. Trusted. Respected. Action taker. Focused. Championing a common goal. These seem to be the things that everyone can agree on. They sound great on paper, but what do they look like, and how does one achieve them?

## Trust

*Any fool with a pulse can earn money.*

*An incompetent with a good work ethic can earn respect.*

*But only an honest and open person can earn trust.*

We were at a client's office, sitting in a room of 12 company employees. The question we had put to them was 'What do you believe to be the biggest roadblocks to the company's growth?'

'The company needs to stand behind its employees', one of the participants said. 'It's frustrating when we're out in the field and have to make a tough decision – then, when a customer gets upset, all they have to do is phone head office, and they will overturn our decision right away.'

It was a topic that had come up the day before when I was talking to the company's senior management team. They recognized that this was a problem and were in the process of taking measures to correct it. However, when I suggested to the assembled group of employees that it was my understanding that this was being addressed, the response was a chorus of derisive laughter. 'Oh, yes,' one employee said, 'they say they're doing lots of things. I'll believe it when I see it. I for one won't be sticking my neck out any more. I don't care if it slows down the process. I'm going to wait and let them make the decisions. At least that way I won't look stupid in front of my customers.'

Here was a company that had completely lost the trust of its employees. The result: lower productivity and lower employee morale.

I'm not sure that there is any more powerful element in an interpersonal relationship than trust. The greater the trust that exists between two people, or within any group of people, the stronger the relationship is. And the stronger an employer–employee relationship, the higher the productivity and job satisfaction. I'm also not sure that there is anything that is harder to win and easier to lose. Many companies try to enhance trust by putting their people through any number of team-building exercises, ranging from the standard lean-back-and-hope-the-person-behind-you-catches-you trust fall to the more extreme rock-climbing and white-water-rafting genre. While these popular events may be enjoyable to some people, and can create a common bonding experience, they usually miss the essence of real trust. The ability to earn trust is less a matter of skill and action than one of character and integrity. When it comes right down to it, earning trust is only a matter of two things: honesty and openness.

I suspect that, if you were to take a poll asking people if they consider themselves to be honest, most, if not all, would respond 'yes'. Yet I would bet a month's salary that almost everyone who answered that question, like the rest of us, is still guilty of telling that little white lie from time to time. We tell the carpet-cleaning telemarketer that we have no carpets in our house. We tell our boss that we're a little further ahead on the project than we really are. We tell our kids that we got higher marks in school than we really did. We tell our friends that the fish we caught was a bit bigger than it really was. We nod politely and tell people we know exactly what they are saying when we really don't have a clue what they are talking about.

For the most part, these little white lies are relatively harmless, and there's no real malice or subterfuge intended. But the problem exists in our different interpretations of where to draw the line. What one person considers to be a little white lie another might see as a damning falsehood.

A person whom I used to work with, for example, who considers herself to have a great deal of integrity, used to be in the habit of making up false pretences in order to bring up certain subjects. 'Oh, while I have you on the line…' was one of her favourite phrases, and she would move from the false pretence to the real reason she'd called.

She wasn't doing anything horrible, but, for those of us who worked with her, we were never quite sure when she brought something up whether it was in fact the topic or whether she had a hidden agenda. The impact of her behaviour was that people became more guarded around her and did not easily take what she said at face value.

Are there any people out there who are totally honest? I believe there are, and I think I even know a few. Shortly after I met my good friend Doug Maguire, now president of Maguire Marketing and Communications, I overheard him telling somebody that he absolutely refused to lie to people. As I do with almost everybody who makes such statements, I took what he said with a hefty grain of salt. 'Oh, yes,' I remember thinking to myself, 'we'll see about that.' That was about 20 years ago, and I'm still waiting to catch him. I often joke with him about how he managed to be so successful in the advertising industry with a silly philosophy like that.

The end result is that I trust Doug absolutely and implicitly. So does everyone else who knows him. I take what he says at face value, and I never question his motives. My 17-year-old son, like Doug, also prides himself on his honesty. And he's finding, as he gets older, that more and more people are prepared to listen to what he has to say because no one questions his words or the motives behind them. As with Doug, I'm still trying to catch him, and to this day I've been unsuccessful. Without the type of unconditional honesty characterized by such people, one will never be able to nurture the kind of trust that is critical to strong leadership.

Tied closely with honesty, and the other key component of earning trust, is the concept of being open with other people. Regardless of how honest you are, if people think information is being withheld from them, there will always be seeds of doubt. As we discussed in the previous chapter, the more information people have, the better. If there is something that you can't tell somebody, you can at least tell that person why.

Allan, a senior manager for a large client of ours, once confided to me his frustration at having been passed over for two promotions that he was very much hoping to get. He assumed that his boss thought he wasn't quite ready for the positions yet, and he was seriously considering moving to another company that would place greater value on his skills and experience.

A few days later, in conversation with the director who was Allan's boss, I discovered that he actually had tremendous regard for Allan's skill as well as his contribution to the company. He had, in fact, a clear and very exciting career path planned for Allan. The two jobs that Allan had been interested in would not have been in his best interests in the medium or long term. The reason that the director hadn't told Allan about his plans was because he hadn't wanted to get his employee's hopes up, just in case things didn't work out. I suggested to him that, while he might not want to tell Allan about his specific plans, he could at least let him know that there was a conscious reason for his not getting the two promotions and that he could hope to get something even better in the near future.

Here was a situation where, while the director had always been completely honest with Allan, his lack of openness in his decision making made Allan question his motives. Openness and honesty. When employees believe they are getting the truth, the whole truth and nothing but the truth, they will begin to trust you.

## Respect

One of the common things you'll hear people say about strong leaders is 'I may not always agree with them, but I really respect them.' In an employer–employee relationship, respect can be divided into two parts: respect for you as a person, and respect for your competence at your job. And, in both cases, being able to earn respect has far more to do with attitude and character than skill. Respect is highly prized, and I've watched some people go through some of the most amazing gyrations to try to get it. Some become workaholics; others become shameless braggarts and self-promoters. Still others try to knock down those around them so they can look better in comparison. But, the fact is, earning people's respect requires none of those things.

Respect is, by nature, a reciprocal thing. Treat other people respectfully, and by and large they will treat you respectfully. Show respect for their professionalism and skill sets, and they will show respect for yours. This is another area in which the telescope effect plays a big role. That is, any action you take with your employee will have a far greater reaction than you expect it will. Walk up to one of your employees some day, pick out something that the employee is exceptional at and say something like 'You know what, Janet? I really admire the way you do that. You're absolutely spectacular at it.' Then watch how the employee responds to you the rest of the day.

## Action

I remember watching author and personal motivation expert Anthony Robbins in a television interview. The host asked him what he considered to be the most common mistake people make in their lives. Robbins's response went something like this: 'People are always saying "Oh, I should have done this; I should have done that. I should have tried this; I should have tried that." Shoulda, shoulda, shoulda. People just "should" all over themselves.'

I couldn't agree more. 'Going to', 'should have', 'would have'. We hear them all the time. 'Yes, we're going to do that soon.' 'Yes, we should have done that, all right.' 'Well, I would have done it, except something else came up.' Most people are far more prepared to talk about things than they are actually to do things. Because of this, action takers stand out from the crowd, and even when we don't agree with their actions we still respect them for their ability and willingness to do them. People admire action takers and follow them. When a team has a boss who keeps them in positive forward motion, they will have greater motivation and thus greater productivity. Being an action taker is critical to effective leadership.

## Focusing on a common goal

Have you ever met one of those people who seem to be able to accomplish absolutely everything they set their minds to? They don't get distracted and don't lose momentum. They are dogged, persistent and relentless. 'Stick-to-it-iveness' my grand-mother used to call it.

Do you remember how you felt when that person was on your side? When that person was on your team or working with you on a project? You felt secure and confident. You thought that, even if things went wrong, that person would be able to fix them. That is exactly the feeling that, as a leader, you want to instil in the people around you.

When employees sense that their manager is seeking the same outcomes that they are, and that the manager is unwavering in his or her conviction, they get a sense of positive motion. And with this sense comes motivation and satisfaction. When employees sense that their manager is unfocused, however, these things are replaced with feelings of anxiety and indif-ference. There is inertia and a general unwillingness to be proactive. Who wants to put his or her job on the line for a project when the manager doesn't really seem to care?

Years ago my company was asked by one of our clients to build a comprehensive set of customer service policies and procedures for a new concept the client had developed. The manager responsible for the project threw everything she had at it – heart and soul. She was excited about the vision created by her superiors and completely dedicated herself to it. The company had allocated substantial financial resources to the project and claimed to be committed to a five-year building process. It was going to set a radical new standard for customer service in the retail industry.

Everything was on track and going according to plan. All of the deliverables were being delivered, and the customer response was tremendous. Nine months later, however, without warning, the company completely removed the funding and began to distance itself from the project. It had decided that five years was too long to wait. The manager was left hanging on a limb, with the 'failed' project sitting squarely on her shoulders. She went on stress leave shortly afterwards and left the company a year later. 'It's what you get for jumping into projects with both feet around here – you always get hurt', one of her colleagues later confided in me. 'Me, I don't take ownership of anything any more.'

I have heard the same sentiment more times than I dare to count. Typically, it stems from the middle management levels of large corporations. The ripple effect from changes made at the shareholder or senior management level, even the little changes, creates a constant state of flux for the people within the company. In these kinds of environments, it is even more critical that employees perceive their managers as being strong leaders.

## Championing employees

Employees also need to believe that, as long as they do their jobs to the best of their abilities, their boss will stand behind them. Loyalty, like respect, is earned – and it begins with you. I once watched the managing director of a London company loudly and violently read the riot act to a secretary who'd apparently botched a FedEx shipment to a client. The manager whom the secretary reported to stepped between them and said to the MD in a quiet but no-nonsense voice 'Hold on. This woman has sweated blood for this company for the past six years. She has saved both of our necks more times than I can count. I don't care what she may or may not have done, she doesn't deserve to be talked to like that. If you want to shout at somebody, shout at me.'

The silence in the room seemed to hang for a lifetime, and then the angry director turned and stormed off.

'Thank you', the appreciative secretary said.

'No problem,' the manager grinned, 'but if I get fired because of this I'm coming over to live at your house.'

'Any time', she replied.

Do you think that this secretary felt more than a little loyalty to her boss? I'm sure she did. There is no better feeling than having your boss stand up for you.

One comment that you will consistently hear from employees who have a high degree of job satisfaction is that they believe their boss will do anything for them. They feel valued, and they know that their boss genuinely cares about them. If you ever get the impression that the loyalty of your employees is beginning to wane, ask yourself what you might be doing to cause the decline.

## Championing the company

Part of the schizophrenia of management is that, while you always need to champion your employees, you also have to champion your company. One trap that managers often fall into is to say negative things about their companies, their bosses or the projects on which their employees are working.

'Yes, it's flavour-of-the-month time', the regional manager of a large distiller once told me as he walked into the seminar room filled with his employees. 'So,' he said with his hands on his hips, 'what's the topic today?' He went on to say that, while his company spent a lot of time and money on training, it never walked the talk. 'This company just loves to flush money down the toilet', he said sarcastically. How much loyalty do you suppose this regional manager's employees had to the company? How much respect for or confidence in the company's direction and decisions were they likely to have?

If a manager puts the company down, what do you suppose the manager's employees do? A large part of your responsibility as a manager is to look for the positives in the company and to make sure that your employees perceive you as being both loyal and dedicated. If they think you don't believe in the company, then they will never feel the need to be loyal themselves.

Want to be a great boss? Develop your leadership skills. Build trust and respect. Focus on a common goal. Take action. Always remember to champion both your employees and your company.

# 4

# Setting immutable performance standards

*You need to determine what is truly important to you and the company, identify exactly what the minimum acceptable level of performance is, communicate it to your employees and then accept nothing less – ever.*

We've all grown up with rules and consequences. They permeate virtually every aspect of our lives. If you drive over the speed limit, you get a ticket. If you commit a crime, you go to jail. Our lives have boundaries, and we all have expectations placed on us. So why is it that so few managers are comfortable setting unwavering standards for their employees?

A lot of performance-related issues with Employees from Hell can be averted by the implementation of performance standards. Standards that are binding and universal. Standards that are immutable.

Every now and then, when I'm presenting to a group of managers, I walk in with a small flagpole. I tell them that the pole represents performance and that the flag represents their team. I ask them how high they would like their flag to be. The answer, inevitably, is all the way to the top. So I make a big show of hoisting the flag to the top of the pole and then stand there holding it while I ask them if this is exactly where they want it. After they have all agreed that the flag is in the right place, I let go of it and walk away from the pole. The flag, of course, falls to the floor. 'Is it still where you want it to be?' I ask. When the group responds with 'No', I say 'So, what? Are you expecting me to stand here through my whole speech holding this stupid thing?' Eventually, someone calls out that maybe I should tape it up there, which I do.

The point I make is that we can boost performance and productivity as much as we want, but if there is no mechanism in place to maintain them they will inevitably fall back down. It is the difference between attaining a goal and setting a standard. A goal can be a one-time thing, while a standard is a constant. As soon as the flag falls, even by a fraction of an inch, the standard ceases to exist. No matter what the circumstances, you can't have a 'flexible standard' – that's an oxymoron.

A standard is a benchmark, an unchanging point from which things can be measured. In golf, it's called 'par'. While most people like to have standards, few of us are adept at setting and maintaining them. Want to watch a real example of someone self-destructing when it comes to performance standards? Go to any beach, walk through any shopping centre or go to a restaurant, and you stand a good chance of witnessing at least one parent in the process of completely undermining any hope of setting standards for his or her children. 'Johnny, don't do that!' the parent will say and then watch Johnny go ahead and do it anyway. 'Suzy, put that back!' will come the reprimand. Only Suzy never has to put it back. 'No, I'm not going to buy you an ice cream!' the parent vows – but, five minutes later, there's the child with the ice cream. No, overall, we're not very good at setting standards.

Although most of us as managers don't like to admit it, we do the same thing with our employees. We give our salespeople targets yet don't apply consequences when they don't meet them. We give deadlines for projects but calmly listen to the whooshing sound as the deadlines blow by. Employees who don't meet the supposed standard get the message loud and clear that you don't really mean what you say. And employees who do meet the standard get the message that they worked far harder than they had to.

Setting immutable standards for the performance of your employees is a critical first step to eliminating difficult situations with employees. You need to determine what is truly important to you and the company, identify exactly what the minimum acceptable level of performance is, communicate it to your employees and then accept nothing less – ever.

# The principles of immutable performance standards

## 1. Stick to the important things

Remember that these are performance standards – not a job description, a procedure manual or a wish list. If it isn't critical to the ongoing success of your business, don't make it a standard. For example, having someone answer the telephone through the Christmas season with 'Season's greetings. This is Veronica speaking. How may I help you?' may be a great idea, but it probably isn't critical to the success of your business. Ensuring that the telephone is always answered with a positive, upbeat tone of voice, however, may be.

## 2. Keep them simple

A company should never have a list of performance standards longer than the employees can easily memorize. Try not to exceed seven. They should be worded in such a way that the meaning of each is clear. Along with keeping them simple, make sure that each standard is specific and single-minded. For example, 'All sales activity will be duly noted on the reporting log, and faxed in to the office, with a follow-up phone call to the customer the next day to confirm the products and quantities' is convoluted and really involves two separate standards – one involving the reporting log, and the other involving customer follow-up.

## 3. Make them universal

A performance standard must apply to everyone on the team or in the group. If your team involves cross-functional work groups, then you might want to consider having one set of three to five performance standards that apply to the entire group and two to three that apply to each subgroup.

## 4. Make them fair

A standard has to be something that everyone on your team can reasonably be expected to maintain. You might have one gung-ho sales rep who works 90 hours a week and makes 100 cold calls a day. As much as you would love to use that person's numbers for the standard within the company, they probably aren't fair or realistic for sales reps who have families at home or some other life to lead.

## 5. Make them a source of pride

In our company, we have a participant feedback form we hand out at the end of a seminar, workshop or clinic. Among other things, we ask the participants how well they liked the programme presentation and how confident they were that the material would be helpful to them. We have a minimum acceptable standard for the first of 4.7 out of 5 and a 98 per cent confidence level for the second. This is a source of much pride for our team, and we take it personally when, for some reason, the numbers fall below those standards.

Once you have introduced performance standards into your workplace, and once they are being met, don't hesitate to toot your horn a little. Encourage your employees to do the same. The sense of pride and accomplishment plays a large role in the team's ongoing motivation.

## 6. Make them measurable

The only way you can effectively get a group of people fully to understand the level of performance expected of them, and collectively and permanently to change their behaviours, is constantly to measure their performance against the standards you've set.

Garth Mitchell, former managing director of a chain of clothes shops, once told me of his company's success: 'We measure everything. Because what gets measured gets done.' It is hard to argue with the company's track record, which is excellent. I have since heard the same sentiment echoed by dozens of other successful companies. What gets measured gets done. One of the things I've discovered, in fact, is that, if it can't be measured, it probably isn't very important.

# Positive and negative consequences

As a manager, you have three basic choices. You can ignore performance standards and just keep lifting the flag up and letting it fall back down over and over. You can set standards and hover over your employees, micromanaging their every move – holding the virtual flag yourself, as it were. Or you can set positive and negative consequences so that the flag stays up on its own. The first option leaves you vulnerable to countless performance issues. The second dramatically increases your workload and can lead to bitterness and resentment. That leaves us with the third option – using positive and negative consequences to hold the standard in place.

These consequences provide substance to the standards and ensure that the whole team commits to achieving them. The secret, however, is in diligent enforcement. Setting consequences can backfire on you if you don't apply them consistently or fairly. In fact, not properly applying the consequences you have set has consequences of its own. Employees might begin to perceive favouritism or simply weakness on your part. As the consequences begin to fall in their eyes, so do the standards and the corresponding performance.

There are four secrets to making performance standards work:

1. Set out your new performance standards and make sure everyone knows them.
2. Visibly and consistently measure the degree to which the standards are being met.
3. Set out positive and negative consequences that are fair and apply to everybody.
4. Apply the consequences every time you see someone either succeed or fail.

If you successfully implement all of these secrets, you will be astounded at the success you achieve and how few employee performance issues you will encounter.

# 5

# Performance coaching

*Learning to SOAR...*

Coaching is perhaps the single most powerful tool at a manager's disposal for building individual performance, yet few of us do it well or consistently. Despite the length of time that 'coaching' has existed in our modern-day management lexicon, most managers still don't see themselves in that role. They see a manager's role as more administrative and authoritative than as instructional and motivational.

When you really begin to take a look at the Employees from Hell out there, you'll see that the majority of them are ultimately performance-related challenges. Employees either unable or unwilling to do their jobs as they are supposed to be done are frustrating to the point of distraction – in part because you know that, if you were doing their jobs yourself, you'd be doing them a lot better.

A senior sales manager I know once told me of a new sales rep who was driving him mad. His company sells top-of-the-range computer software packages. The sales cycle for their products is extremely long and complex and requires experienced and skilled salespeople. His new sales rep's pipeline of prospective new customers was diminishing quickly, largely because of her inability to think through the cycle.

'In an example of this,' the manager told me, 'she recently dropped a prospect from the pipeline. When I asked where it had gone (it was a university that I had qualified and was one of my pet accounts), she explained that she had sent three e-mails to the contact and that the contact had not responded. Based on this, she had decided that this was a dead account.

'I suggested that she should have read the history of the prospect. The contact's son has cancer, and he is therefore frequently away from the office. He rarely responds to e-mails. The best thing is to phone periodically and catch him during those moments when he's in his office. This contact was quite eager to schedule a meeting. But this rep had not bothered to read through the accumulation of historical information we had on the university.'

The sales manager knew what had to be done. He knew that, if he were to take over, he would be able to make the sale, and he couldn't understand why the answer wasn't as obvious to her as it was to him. But he also knew that his sales rep would never improve in the long run if he didn't at least try to help her understand.

Sound familiar? Consider some of the following:

- the administrative assistant who is completely unorganized;
- the employee who never adopts new procedures without a fight;
- the salesperson who simply won't ask enough discovery questions;
- the telephone customer service representative who continues to challenge and scold customers;
- the warehouse employee who won't pick up the pace;
- the middle manager who won't change his or her management style;
- the service person who is rude to customers;
- the receptionist who sounds bored over the telephone.

These are all performance issues. And the good news is that most of them can be corrected through performance coaching.

A lot of people get training, mentoring and coaching confused. In a nutshell, here's the difference. Training is the process of transferring new knowledge, skills or perspectives to someone. Mentoring is the process of providing additional knowledge, skills and perspectives to someone on an ongoing basis – usually in a live environment. Coaching is the process of assisting and encouraging people to apply knowledge, skills and perspectives consistently in a live environment.

I can't count the number of times I've heard a manager grumble something like 'I must have told them a hundred times not to do it that way.'

My answer is always the same. 'So why do you suppose it's not sinking in?'

And their response to me is usually the same as well. 'I have no idea.'

'Well, maybe it's time you found out.'

Simply telling people something has little impact on performance. For starters, we humans don't really listen very well. But, more importantly, we don't change our behaviours and actions easily. To replace an old habit, we have to work on creating a new one, and that requires practice, drills and rehearsal. That's what coaching is all about.

Hardly a week goes by without us encountering a highly skilled employee who thinks that he or she isn't getting anywhere. Almost always this frustration is a result of a lack of consistent, focused direction and encouragement on the part of the employee's manager. As managers, we often get so caught up with the daily operations of our little worlds that we lose sight of developing our most important assets – our employees. Performance coaching involves four basic steps that, as fortune would have it, create the acronym **SOAR**:

**S**et goals.
**O**bserve performance.
**A**ssess performance.
**R**espond appropriately.

The elements are straightforward and relatively easy to execute. The biggest challenge is to execute them consistently. The pay-off in employee performance, productivity and satisfaction, however, makes it all worthwhile. Ken Blanchard and Spencer Johnson illustrated many years ago in *The One-Minute Manager* that assisting and encouraging employees to rise to new levels of performance and job satisfaction don't have to take a great deal of time, but they do take commitment.

# 6

# Setting goals

*You should always work on the assumption that employees can't read your mind.*

Once upon a time, there was a man who decided he wanted to be the best racing car driver ever. He started by setting out to build an amazing racing car. He spent months seeking out the sleekest, lightest, most aerodynamic body ever developed. He spent a small fortune on the best engine, drivetrain and tyres money could buy. Then he took driving lessons from the best racing instructors in the business. But, despite all his investments of time and money, he never won a single race. You see, while he was always much faster and more skilled than anybody else on the track, he never seemed to be quite sure where he was going. The same thing can happen with skilled and motivated employees.

Performance failures are very often followed by the words 'But I thought you wanted me to...' Sometimes employees aren't quite sure what is expected of them. Their negative behaviour often stems from frustration over insufficient or unclear direction.

Performance coaching begins with making sure that employees are perfectly clear each day on what your expectations are of them. If you want to assist and encourage people to improve their performance, the first step is to set goals for them.

Daily goals. Goals that are challenging, attainable, measurable and tangible. Goals that give them the satisfaction of a job well done at the end of the day.

Begin by creating for yourself a daily coaching log, like the one in Figure 6.1. (If you wish, you can download one free from my company's website, www.beldingskills.com, or you can contact our office and have one e-mailed to you.) A coaching log provides you with a reference point and a record for your coaching endeavours. It begins with setting daily goals.

Every morning, for each employee, pick an area where you would like to see that employee develop. In no more than one minute, let the employee know exactly what his or her daily development goal is, and make sure the employee understands precisely how you define successful achievement of that goal. Write it down in the log, and have the employee initial the objective to confirm that you both have the same understanding of it. Make goal setting part of your daily routine. It's not time-consuming at one minute per person, and the results will astonish you and your employees. Productivity will increase, along with employee satisfaction. The better direction you are giving, the more races you will win, and the more races you win, the better everyone feels.

# Principles of setting performance goals

## 1. Make them relevant

If you haven't done so already, carefully analyse your business and create a comprehensive master list of all the skills and behaviours employees need to be successful at their jobs. Make a list of all the areas in which you would like to see your employees develop. Focus on skills and attitudes, not on tasks. It is not an easy process, but it is a valuable one.

**COACHING LOG**

Employee: _____
Coach: _____

BELDING
SKILLS DEVELOPMENT CORPORATION
USA – Canada: 1-800-661-7927

| OBJECTIVES | OBSERVATIONS | ASSESSMENT | RESPONSE |
|---|---|---|---|
| Date: | | Achieved the Objective | |
| | | Approached the Objective | |
| | | Did not Achieve the Objective | |

| OBJECTIVES | OBSERVATIONS | ASSESSMENT | RESPONSE |
|---|---|---|---|
| Date: | | Achieved the Objective | |
| | | Approached the Objective | |
| | | Did not Achieve the Objective | |

| OBJECTIVES | OBSERVATIONS | ASSESSMENT | RESPONSE |
|---|---|---|---|
| Date: | | Achieved the Objective | |
| | | Approached the Objective | |
| | | Did not Achieve the Objective | |

| OBJECTIVES | OBSERVATIONS | ASSESSMENT | RESPONSE |
|---|---|---|---|
| Date: | | Achieved the Objective | |
| | | Approached the Objective | |
| | | Did not Achieve the Objective | |

| OBJECTIVES | OBSERVATIONS | ASSESSMENT | RESPONSE |
|---|---|---|---|
| Date: | | Achieved the Objective | |
| | | Approached the Objective | |
| | | Did not Achieve the Objective | |

Copyright 2003, Belding Skills Development Corportation

**Figure 6.1** Daily coaching log

Once you have created a skills map, the process of guiding an employee to higher performance levels becomes much easier. A skills map is created by breaking skills down to their basic components and then systematically breaking the components down into smaller and smaller pieces. The smallest pieces make up your bank of coaching goals.

Figure 6.2 is an example of how a skill can be broken down into daily coaching goals. This illustration shows how the discovery process, one of the key skills of selling, can be broken down into progressively smaller elements. The thread identified in the sample chart shows how the skill of discovery can be drilled down through its subcomponents – listening, prompting, word choice, vocabulary and gentle language.

When this process is repeated for each component of the discovery process, you will discover over a hundred distinct

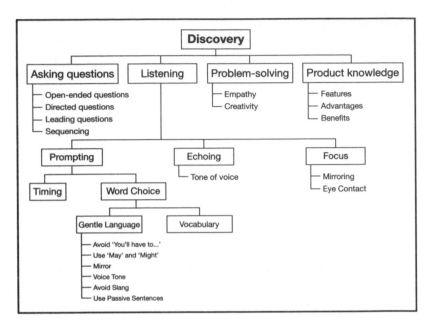

**Figure 6.2** Breaking a skill down into daily coaching goals

things that can be used for daily coaching goals. The same will be found from mapping out virtually all workplace skills.

By mining and mapping each skill, you will be able to ensure that the objectives you set each day are relevant to developing each employee and that you are proceeding in a logical, productive manner.

## 2. Keep them simple

The simpler, the better. Now, by simpler, of course, I don't mean easier – I mean single-minded and focused. If you make a performance goal too complex, or if you give someone too many goals at a time, you hinder the employee's ability to understand it and achieve success.

## 3. Make them attainable

There used to be a philosophy that, if you can keep the goal just slightly out of reach, you will be able to motivate people to do great things – much like the old practice of dangling carrots in front of horses' noses. Unfortunately, with humans, that process just leads to frustration and bitterness.

When you set a goal for an employee, make sure that it is attainable for him or her. It doesn't matter if the employee's colleague can achieve it easily. If the person you are coaching can't do it, it will only frustrate him or her.

I remember conducting a coaching session with four employees in a department store. One of the goals was to try to have the employees change from their standard 'Can I help you?' question to the more productive 'What can I help you find today?' and similar questions. Halfway through the session, three of the four employees had begun to make the change fairly consistently. The fourth, however, kept faltering badly, and it became apparent that she would be unable to achieve the goal.

As it turned out, it wasn't the change in wording that was creating the challenge. This employee simply wasn't used to the idea of initiating contact with customers in the first place. Until she became comfortable doing that, she would never become comfortable with the change in wording. We had to change her goal.

We reset it for her to 'greet every customer who comes through the door with a smile and hello'. She achieved it after a lot of effort and went home with a feeling of accomplishment. How would she have felt, though, if we hadn't changed her goal and she hadn't achieved it? The failure would have dealt a tremendous blow to her self-esteem and motivation.

## 4. Make them challenging

Attainability isn't the only thing that makes a goal motivating. It also has to be challenging. Telling someone to stand there and breathe, for example, is attainable, but the person isn't likely to have a great and rewarding sense of accomplishment.

The purpose of coaching is to help people develop their skill sets. This means that the goal you set has to push their limits, either by introducing new skills or by encouraging them to use existing skills more consistently. Simply reinforcing a skill that someone has already mastered will be unproductive at best and has the potential to be counter-productive.

The wife of a friend of mine is a computer programmer in a very specialized field. She happens to be very good at what she does in relation to the people around her, so, when her boss sets goals, she usually has them completed halfway through the day. After repeatedly and unsuccessfully asking for something more challenging, she now spends her downtime working on a website for her personal home business. Is she an Employee from Hell? Technically, yes. She is using company resources and time for personal use. Practically, however, she is not. She is simply looking for some productive way to use her time. Were her boss to find something a bit more challenging for her, everyone would be a winner.

## 5. Communicate their importance

Have you ever had someone give you what you consider to be just a 'make-work project'? Do you remember how demotivating it was? When people don't understand or appreciate the importance of their work, they begin to question your assessment of their importance to the company. As we discussed in Chapter 3, respect is a mutual thing, and, when an employee begins feeling that you don't respect him or her, challenges can develop.

In that one-minute period when you are outlining the performance goals for the day, be clear about why achieving the goals is important. Let's say you are a supervisor in a call centre, and the goal you have set for one of your employees is to finish every call with 'Is there anything else I can do for you?' You might present the goal to your employee like this:

Here's what I'd like you to concentrate on today. At the end of every call, say to the customer 'Is there anything else I can do for you?' We're focusing on this because it reinforces to customers that they are important to you, and it might trigger something that could save them another phone call and us opening up another ticket. Will you give that a try today?

In this instance, the employee now has two reasons to adopt the new language. First, it will send a positive message to the customer; second, it might make life easier for him- or herself or a colleague. The employee is satisfied that the goal wasn't set just for the sake of setting a goal and that there is an important purpose behind it.

## 6. Give them time frames

Any goal you give to someone needs to have a time frame. Most of us work better when we know there's a deadline. It's particularly important to set time frames for performance goals, because they are typically situation based. They're based on interaction with and response to other things and people. Let's say you set for yourself the non-performance goal of cleaning up your work area by Friday afternoon. The goal is a good one, but the Friday afternoon part is not necessary to achieving it. You might have it done on Thursday afternoon or Friday morning. Even if you get it done by Saturday morning, you will still have a sense of accomplishment.

Performance goals, however, revolve around situations. 'When a customer calls, I will maintain a bright tone to my voice.' 'When a customer walks in the door, I will smile.' 'When we're in a brainstorming meeting, I will use only positive language.' Your goal is tied to something or somebody else.

What this means is that simply saying 'I want you to smile at your customers' isn't good enough. You need to make it clear: 'I want you to smile at every customer when they walk in the door.' This tells your employee exactly what you are expecting and when you are expecting it.

One of the most common mistakes that we as managers make is to assume that our employees understand the things we want them to do. We assume that they will prioritize things the same way we will. We assume that they will think through challenges the same way we do. You are always better off assuming the opposite. It doesn't mean that they're stupid; it just means that you should always work on the assumption that they can't read your mind. Your best bet is to spend one minute each day with each of your employees and set clear, concise, motivating goals for them. You will find that productivity will go up and that your employees will be much more comfortable and confident in knowing what you expect of them.

The key to setting goals, again, is to make sure they are relevant, simple, attainable and challenging. Give them a time-frame, and make sure that your employee understands their importance.

# 7

# Observing performance

*It takes neither courage, nor imagination, nor brains to find problems. Problems have a way of finding us.*

OK, so, like a good coach, you've outlined the game plan for the day. The team members are reminded of their roles and their individual performance goals. It's time for the work to commence and the game to begin. Like your counterparts in football, rugby, hockey, tennis and cricket, your job is now to stand on the sidelines and watch each player perform. There are three key rules to observing performance and one important trap to avoid.

## **Rule 1**: Look for the good first

One of my favourite questions to ask a group of managers is 'When you return to the work environment after a couple of days' absence, what do you look for first – what's going right or what's going wrong?' I like the question for two reasons. First, the response is much the same every time – people look for the things that aren't quite right. Second, the look on people's faces is also the same – a little sheepish. We all know what the right answer should be. We've all heard the theory of how important 'catching someone doing something right' is. But we are all still human, and human nature is to look for the negatives first.

Looking for positives, for things that are going right, requires conscious effort and discipline. You have to want to find positives, and you have to be prepared to attune yourself to them. Remember, it takes neither courage, nor imagination, nor brains to find problems. Problems have a way of finding us.

## **Rule 2**: Be open

Observing your employees shouldn't be a covert operation. Quite the opposite, in fact. All team members should be aware that you will be monitoring their performance. If you set performance goals for them, and they sense that you aren't monitoring how well they are doing, they will probably assume that the goals weren't really important and that you don't really care.

## **Rule 3**: Be discreet

Although you want to be open about your performance monitoring, you should never be in the way or so obvious that you are making people nervous. Don't hover or stare. I remember once watching an overzealous retail assistant manager trying to coach his staff for the first time. He was following the salespeople and customers around so closely that customers were leaving out of sheer discomfort. To make matters worse, he was in the habit of jumping into the sales interviews whenever a salesperson seemed to be faltering.

It's easy to forget that your role at this point is as an observer only. Watching someone struggle when you know you could do a better job isn't easy to do, but it can be devastating if you don't resist the temptation to get involved. Remember the old Chinese proverb: 'Give a man a fish; you feed him for a day.

Teach a man to fish; you feed him for a lifetime.' (Although the wife of a fisherman friend of mine insists that it should be 'Give a man a fish; you feed him for a day. Teach a man to fish, and he'll sit around in a boat drinking beer all weekend.') Be patient with people.

## The trap: Don't lose focus on your objectives

One of the biggest traps managers fall into while coaching is losing focus while observing performance. As you undertake to coach on a consistent basis, you suddenly become much more aware of your employees' performance and behaviour than ever before. You begin to see a great many things in each employee's behaviour that you would like to correct in addition to those related to the objective you have set. The trap is that you lose your focus and try to fix everything right away. We managers are conditioned to respond to negative stimuli – to the exceptions. And, as we encounter more and more things that need to be corrected, the urge to take immediate action can be overwhelming. While your increasing awareness of your employees and their performance is a good thing, it is critical that you don't try to correct issues outside the specific goals you have set.

It will be tremendously unfair to your employees if you set one objective for them and then evaluate them on another. Not only will you instantly undo any good the coaching has done, but you'll also risk losing your employees' respect and trust. Think about a football coach sending players out with explicit instructions to mark specific opposing players. If the players go out and do so to the best of their ability, they won't appreciate being criticized by the coach for not tackling other players – even if the opportunity to do so was right in front of them. The players were focused on the objective set by the coach, and that is the objective the coach should be focused on as well. When you begin to see additional behaviours that you think may require coaching, write them down. You can use your skills map to identify where they belong and then set them as future objectives.

The observation part of the process involves monitoring and shadowing. It is passive and non-participatory. Going back to the telescope effect, it is important to recognize the great amount of discomfort that your employees will initially have as you observe them. The good news, however, is that, once your employees get comfortable with the idea and they see that you are consistent and fair, they will actually look forward to having you watch their work.

Here again are the three rules for effective observation and the one trap to avoid:

- Rule 1: Look for the good first.
- Rule 2: Be open.
- Rule 3: Be discreet.
- The trap: Don't lose your focus.

# 8

# Assessing performance

*You can't evaluate one person based on the abilities of another.*

You've set the objective for the day, and you've observed your employee in action. The next step is to determine the degree to which the objective was met. It is important that, before you respond to what you've seen, you take the time to assess the information you've gathered. There are two basic questions you have to answer:

1. Did the employee make a visible effort to achieve the objective?
2. Did the employee succeed in meeting the objective?

The answer to the first question will be somewhat subjective. Different employees master skills at different rates, and the same effort put in by any two will generate varying results. Let's say you give employees Bill and Chris the goal of 'giving every customer whom you encounter a warm, genuine smile'. Bill, a naturally outgoing and expressive person, accomplishes this goal easily. Chris, a more shy and introverted person, forces a small but awkward smile – kind of like he's got wind. When it comes to the analysis, how do you rate Chris? In comparison to Bill, Chris failed miserably. But in relation to his own current abilities and comfort level, his effort may actually have exceeded Bill's. The answer is that, while Chris may not have quite achieved the objective, he certainly made an effort. The lesson? You can't evaluate one person based on the abilities of another.

As with the observation process, it is also important not to fall into the common trap of assessing performance that wasn't part of the original objective. Using the example above, if the employee succeeds in smiling more but makes poor eye contact while doing so, don't take the eye contact into consideration in your assessment. You can make note of it as a future objective, but it would be both unfair and demotivating to address it during the current coaching session.

An employee's performance will fall into one of three categories:

1.  achieved the goal;
2.  approached the goal; or
3.  did not achieve the goal.

The first category, 'achieved the goal', is pretty straightforward. Your employee has done everything you asked him or her to do precisely the way you asked it to be done. In the second category, 'approached the goal', your employee has made an effort but hasn't quite achieved the goal as outlined – like the almost-smiling Chris in our earlier example. And, in the third category, 'did not achieve the goal', your employee has made no visible effort to achieve the goal.

## Avoid preconceptions

The biggest challenge in assessing our employees' behaviour is first accepting and then dealing with our own lack of objectivity. Because these might be employees with whom you have worked for some time, you could have preconceived notions about how they will perform and the areas in which they will struggle. You know that Frank isn't a good team player; you know that Rachel tends to be abrupt on the telephone; you know that Bill can't close a sale. The problem is that these preconceptions can actually hinder our ability to recognize performance levels and improvements.

I've been involved with coaching in young people's sports for a long time as a parent, a coach and more recently a volunteer teaching coaches how to motivate their teams more effectively. Every year players compete for various sides, and coaches have to determine where to place each of them. As always, the hardest part comes down to evaluating that last group of seven or eight players vying for the final few places. This last group is always the hardest to evaluate because they are typically very close in skill level. It's interesting to listen to the coaches trying to come to a decision about this group: each sees different things, and those who know some of the players from the year before already have preconceptions. Players get labelled and have great difficulty breaking through the barriers that those labels create.

I remember in particular a discussion about one young man trying out for the local football team. He'd been at various levels in the league for six years. He was a nice, quiet young man who played a steady, solid game. All of the coaches liked him, but there was one concern.

'He's a good player,' one coach put it, 'but he's never been very physical, and it's a pretty rough game at this level. I'm not sure he'll be able to handle it.'

Heads around the room, including mine, nodded in agreement.

Then a lone dissenter spoke. 'I don't know him as well as you all do, I suppose,' he said, 'but, according to the records, he's delivered more tackles than almost anyone else in the last few games. It looks to me as though he's a strong player. It doesn't look as though he's going to have a challenge.'

We all looked at the team sheets again and discovered, to our astonishment, that he was right. Rather than evaluating his current performance, we were evaluating his past performance.

When you are assessing an employee's performance, give serious thought to your assessment. Try, as much as possible, to remain open-minded. Be aware of your preconceptions, and be prepared to question your own objectivity. Keep in mind that people do have the ability to change behaviour, but you'll never know if you don't look for it.

Remember that employees' performance will fall into one of three categories: they achieved the goal, they approached the goal or they did not achieve the goal.

# 9

# Responding to performance

*Imagine what the work environment would be like if all the managers you know allocated just 20 minutes a day to do this with all their employees.*

The final and most critical element of the coaching process is the way in which you respond to your employees' performance. This is the most challenging stage and, not surprisingly, the one that most managers execute the least well. Most managers, when faced with employees who are not performing to standard, either ignore the problem and hope it magically corrects itself or come down too hard on the employee, creating resentment and demotivation. Similarly, when employees achieve their goals, their managers often say nothing, or as good as nothing, leaving employees wondering why they tried so hard in the first place.

The response to an employee's performance should come immediately after his or her attempts at achieving the goal. Don't wait for the end of the week or even the end of the day. As undignified as the analogy seems, it's rather like training a dog. As soon as the dog makes a mess on the carpet, you put its nose beside it and say 'Bad dog'. If you wait until the end of the day to say 'Bad dog', it won't have any idea what you're referring to. Although most of us are typically a little more sophisticated than dogs, things are still more meaningful to us when they are fresh in our memories.

As a general rule, you should try to respond to your employees as soon as possible after they have attempted to achieve the goal. If the employee is a retail salesperson, take a few moments to talk to him or her as soon as the customer has left. If the employee works in a call centre, you can talk to him or her as soon as the call is over. If the employee is a manager, you can talk to him or her as soon as the meeting is over. During the course of a day, you may respond several times to your employees' performance.

Now, you might be thinking that this whole process is just going to take far too much time. The truth is, it does take time – but not as much as you might think. Most coaching responses should take no more than a minute when done right. Considering the payback of using positive coaching techniques, it is often the best investment of your time.

As we discussed in Chapter 8, when you assess employees' performance based on the objectives you set, there are really only three possible outcomes – they succeeded completely, they gave it a good try but didn't succeed 100 per cent or they failed completely.

Correspondingly, there are three types of responses to performance: positive, constructive and corrective.

# 1. The positive response

When your employee has achieved the goal in full, your response must be unequivocally and absolutely positive. After you have responded, there should be no doubt in the employee's mind that he or she was successful.

You might think that this is rather obvious. It is. The only challenge is that most of us just don't do positive reinforcement and praise very well. Oh, certainly, sometimes we'll give an employee a mumbled 'Good job', but we rarely take advantage of the opportunity to really motivate a high-performing employee. Many bosses, even when praising their employees, can't seem to resist counterbalancing it with something negative. 'That's great', I heard a CEO once say to one of his managers. 'Too bad you didn't do that on the last project.'

There seems to be some unwritten rule somewhere that managers are supposed to keep their positive emotions in check, that approval and praise are somehow signs of weakness that will compromise our abilities to manage. Several managers have told me that they don't like to give too much praise because employees will then expect more money. Not coincidentally, these managers seem to have more Employees from Hell and a much greater rate of employee turnover than the norm.

When employees make the effort and achieve a goal set out for them, this is the time to step outside our typically conservative comfort zones and really demonstrate our appreciation of their performance. Say 'Excellent!' 'Wonderful!' 'That's terrific!' Show your enthusiasm. The pay-off is huge. You get employees who feel valued and are motivated to maintain that level of performance. It's an attitude that is infectious and can spread through the entire team.

The cost of not responding positively is equally huge. Many Employees from Hell whom I have met are basically nice people who have simply given up. 'Why should I care?' they ask me. 'My boss doesn't.' Try being more positive. I have never once heard employees complain that the boss compliments them too much.

## 2. The constructive response

It would be wonderful if your employees achieved their goals 100 per cent every day. Chances are good, though, that this won't happen – particularly if you have ensured that the goals are challenging. The most common scenario is that an employee will attempt to achieve the goal but will not quite achieve 100 per cent success or consistency. It is with these, the majority of your employees, that coaching has the most dramatic effect on performance. These are the ones who have demonstrated a willingness to try, but need the assistance and encouragement that you can provide to master the skill.

When employees have made an attempt to attain a goal, but haven't quite met it, two things are important. First, you have to acknowledge their effort. They need reassurance that you know they are trying. Second, they need your guidance and encouragement to continue trying until they do meet their objectives. Achieving both of these outcomes requires careful attention to our language skills and the ways in which we present ourselves. The best way that I know of to accomplish this is a 'good stuff–bad stuff–good stuff' format. Once you've mastered its execution, you will discover that it has a wide range of applications and that it works amazingly well. It has six steps.

## The good stuff–bad stuff–good stuff format

Let me illustrate how this is executed. Your employee is Linda, a receptionist who is very efficient but often comes across to customers as being abrupt and cold. The goal you have set for her is to 'Look up and smile at everyone who comes into the office'. She begins well and wins over the first eight customers with a dazzling smile and clear eye contact. The ninth, however, is a Customer from Hell who loudly and rudely complains about the company and berates her abilities to get things done. After this, a shaken Linda forgets about her goal and falls back into her old habits.

### 1. Begin with the employee's point of view

The first step is to approach your employee and find out how well she thinks she's doing. In our example, you would look for a quiet time to walk up to Linda and say 'How are you doing with the smiling so far?'

You ask her first because she may already be aware that she has slid back into her old habits. She may respond with 'I was doing well at first – until that Customer from Hell walked in. I honestly haven't been trying very hard since then.' If she acknowledges her failure to meet her goal, then your only task at hand is to pick her up, dust her off and encourage her to keep trying.

If you don't ask for her perspective and instead just start pointing out things she's already aware of, you run the risk of irritating her. Imagine accidentally tearing up a winning lottery ticket, only to have your friend say 'That was really stupid – you could have been rich if you hadn't done that.' Now, not only do you feel stupid, but your friend is also rubbing it in. The last thing you want to do is demotivate someone who is already down on herself. What most of us would like our friends to say instead is something like 'I feel so bad for you! Don't worry about it; it just means that the next one you win will be bigger!'

Most often, however, employees are unable either to recognize or to acknowledge the failure to meet their objectives. It's not because they're stupid or unaware – it's just very difficult for people to be objective when it comes to their own performance. When this happens – when your employee responds to your question with something like 'I think I'm doing pretty well' – you move on to the next part of the good stuff–bad stuff–good stuff format.

## 2. Tell her the good stuff

It doesn't matter how open-minded or rational a person is; nobody likes the feeling of being criticized. This is particularly true when the critic is the person who does your annual performance appraisal. People's responses to criticism can vary from defensiveness to denial to outright aggression. Few of us respond very positively.

It is thus important that you begin by letting your employee know that you respect her and that you appreciate the effort she has made in trying to attain the performance goal. Remember that, in this instance, the employee has given it a real effort but just hasn't quite succeeded yet. So start off by letting her know that you saw her doing some things right.

Make sure that what you say is genuine and relevant to the performance goals you set. To refer to our example, it may go something like the following:

> You: How are you doing with the smiling so far?
> Linda: Pretty well, I think.
> You: Well, I was able to watch you with the first few people. You were fabulous! You really lit the room up. I don't know if you noticed or not, but I did – the customers really liked you!

Don't be afraid to lay the positive stuff on thickly. While you might find it a little over the top while you're doing it, you'll be surprised at how positively your employee will respond. Again, I have never heard anyone complain that his or her boss was too complimentary.

## 3. Tell her the bad stuff

The next step is to introduce the area where your employee still needs to improve. Needless to say, how you introduce it is paramount to your success. The telescope effect plays a role here too. Remember that the slightest criticism from you, as the boss, is likely to land much harder than you intended. It means that your choice of language in presenting the areas that need addressing must be as gentle as you can make it, without running the risk of being wishy-washy. It also means avoiding, at all costs, the words 'however', 'but' and 'although'.

We all know what 'but' means when it follows a compliment. It means 'Ignore everything I've just said, because I'm just about to tell you what I really mean.' It is a killer.

As you try to execute the good stuff–bad stuff–good stuff format, you will find this part to be by far the most difficult. The temptation to use one of those three words will be overwhelming. Because most people aren't used to communicating in a more positive manner, we struggle when trying to find alternatives. You should think through what you're going to say and how you're going to say it before you begin the response. You don't want to undo all of the good you've initiated.

**Figure 9.1** Words to avoid

## 4. Get your employee's agreement

Before you move on, ensure that your employee agrees with your assessment. If, after you point out the area in which she still needs to improve, she still does not agree, you might have to re-examine your assessment with her. You might have heard something wrongly or seen something out of context. Or your employee might be unwilling to face up to the truth, in which case you might have to be a bit more forceful with your point of view.

Let's take a look at how you can word the bad stuff and gain agreement using our example:

> *You: How are you doing with the smiling so far?*
> Linda: Pretty well, I think.
> *You: Well, I was able to watch you with the first few people. You were fabulous! You really lit the room up. I don't know if you noticed or not, but I did – the customers really liked you!*
> Linda: Thanks!
> *You: Look, that really obnoxious customer you had – he got under your skin a bit, didn't he?*
> Linda: You can say that again.
> *You: Did you notice that after you had to deal with that guy you stopped focusing on smiling a bit?*
> Linda: Yes, I suppose I did.

Here you were able to point out Linda's negative behaviour in such a way that she was comfortable agreeing with your assessment. She didn't feel threatened, and you didn't make her feel stupid. As you know, some people out there become defensive easily, and the language you choose and the tone of voice you use are critical at this stage.

## 5. Reinforce the good stuff

Whatever you do, you absolutely do not want to leave your employee on a sour note – particularly after she has been making a concerted effort to achieve the goal you set for her. As soon as she has admitted to you that she hasn't quite achieved her goal, you need to jump back in with the positive things she has done. Doing so lets her know that, although her performance isn't perfect yet, you still have a great deal of respect for her and believe that she has the capacity to develop. Here's how it looks in the example:

> You: How are you doing with the smiling so far?
> Linda: Pretty well, I think.
> You: Well, I was able to watch you with the first few people. You were fabulous! You really lit the room up. I don't know if you noticed or not, but I did – the customers really liked you!
> Linda: Thanks!
> You: Look, that really obnoxious customer you had – he got under your skin a bit, didn't he?
> Linda: You can say that again.
> You: Did you notice that after you had to deal with that guy you stopped focusing on smiling a bit?
> Linda: Yes, I suppose I did.
> You: That guy was an idiot – don't let him bother you. You were doing such a great job. I'm serious – up until he came along, you were terrific!

Mission accomplished. You have communicated to your employee that you appreciated her effort and saw some good things. You let her know that there are a few areas that she still needs to work on, but that overall you were pleased with her effort. What more would an employee want to hear? You have just set her up for success.

## 6. Gain her commitment to continue

Before you leave your response session, gain your employee's commitment to continue her pursuit of the goal. You don't have to make a big deal of it; you just need to let her know that you'd like her to keep trying. Here is how the complete coaching response might look in our example:

> *You: How are you doing with the smiling so far?*
> Linda: Pretty well, I think.
> *You: Well, I was able to watch you with the first few people. You were fabulous! You really lit the room up. I don't know if you noticed or not, but I did – the customers really liked you!*
> Linda: Thanks!
> *You: Look, that really obnoxious customer you had – he got under your skin a bit, didn't he?*
> Linda: You can say that again.
> *You: Did you notice that after you had to deal with that guy you stopped focusing on smiling a bit?*
> Linda: Yes, I suppose I did.
> *You: That guy was an idiot – don't let him bother you. You were doing such a great job. I'm serious, up until he came along, you were terrific!*
> Linda: Yes.
> *You: Will you keep working on the goal of smiling and eye contact? I can't promise you won't get another customer like that, but it's really making a difference.*
> Linda: I'll make sure I do.

In less than a minute, you were able to acknowledge Linda's efforts, refocus her on the goal, let her know how much you respect her, and get her commitment to keep trying. Her morale is up, and she recognizes the importance of her efforts. Imagine what the work environment would be like if all the managers you know allocated just 20 minutes a day to do this with all their employees.

Most of us want to do well. Most of us make mistakes. Similarly, most of the non-performing employees you encounter, those Employees from Hell who seem to be either unwilling or unable to get the job done right, simply lack skills and encouragement. Practise the constructive response. The pay-off is tremendous. You'll find that, if you can master the constructive response as outlined in this chapter, it will serve you well in a wide variety of situations both at work and in your personal life.

# 3. The corrective response

Occasionally, you will encounter an employee who makes no apparent effort and completely fails to achieve the goal. On these rare occasions, your strategy changes to the corrective response.

You begin by trying to discover why your employee is apparently not trying. It's not a good idea to second-guess your employee. The best way to find out is right from the horse's mouth. Ask the employee directly. 'I've been watching you, and it doesn't look as though you are trying to hit that goal we set out. Is there a reason?' The answer you get will let you know how to proceed from there.

Let's take a look at some of the reasons why one of your employees might be so seemingly blatantly disrespectful as not even to attempt to hit the goal you have set for him or her. There are a number of possible reasons, and not all of them are bad.

## 1. Fear of failure

Many people are uncomfortable trying something new because they lack confidence and are afraid that they might fail. They are afraid that they will look stupid in front of people and that their entire character will be judged based on how well they accomplish the task. Some might actually fear for their jobs. Fear of failure can completely paralyse some people, and it will require a great deal of encouragement on your part to help them take action. The task may be unlike anything they have ever done before, in which case it is fear of the unknown; or it may be that they tried to do it once before and failed.

If it turns out that fear of failure is the reason for inaction, your job now becomes to convince them that the costs of inaction are far greater than the costs of acting and failing. You have to start by acknowledging their fear and showing empathy. Saying things like 'Oh, that's just silly' only makes people feel stupid and reinforces the notion that you really don't understand them. Following your acknowledgement, you have to carefully create a cost–benefit scale so that they can understand how the consequences of not doing something outweigh the consequences of trying and failing.

Let's say that you have a salesperson with the goal of trying to add additional items to every purchase. He has made no effort, and you discover that it is because he is afraid that customers will become upset with him and perceive him as pushy. Here's an example of how you might present the cost–benefit case to him:

> John, I understand exactly how you feel. And you're right – we don't want our customers to become upset with us. What I think you maybe haven't considered, though, is that there are a great many customers who appreciate having the accessories. It saves some of them a second trip because they forgot to purchase them the first time around. It saves others from embarrassment over not knowing enough to have asked for them in the first place. You're working on the assumption that our customers don't want our products. Why not work on the assumption that they do? Of course, some customers are going to say no, but most will understand your asking. Besides, John, this is part of our selling process, and you have to master it eventually.

In this example, the manager acknowledged John's feelings and validated them. The manager then outlined why John changing his behaviour was in the customer's best interest and then, by saying 'you have to master it eventually', let John know that it was a requirement of the job. John now has the clear choice between attempting to achieve the goal and seeking another line of work.

## 2. Misunderstanding the task

Sometimes your employees simply misunderstand what you are asking and will correct their behaviour as soon as they understand the task. In this case, make a point of taking the heat yourself for the misunderstanding. Even if you believe that an employee simply wasn't paying close enough attention, it serves no purpose to make him or her feel stupid. A simple 'I'm sorry about that; I probably didn't explain it very well' clears up the issue.

## 3. Lack of self-awareness

Many times I have heard employees say to their bosses 'I was doing it!' It's amazing how many people are completely unaware of their own behaviour and assume that, just because they know what to do, they are automatically doing it.

In our sales and customer service programmes, we talk about trying to be a little more positive in our response to 'Hello, how are you?' We encourage people to be something a little better than just 'OK' or 'Not too bad' or even 'Good'. Customers' expectations of you will rise if you tell them that you are great, wonderful, terrific, etc.

Occasionally, when we are coaching, we set the goal as 'Tell every customer that you are something better than just good.' It's amazing how many employees are convinced that they are saying something different when they have actually fallen right back into their old habits. One employee, whom I happened to catch on tape saying to a customer 'I'm not too bad', was astonished when I played it back to him later. 'No way', he said. 'That wasn't me!'

In these instances when people are just not aware of their behaviour, you have to become a little less subtle during the observation process so that they begin to recognize their behaviour right away. You might also want to enlist someone to observe with you so that he or she can confirm to the employees what you have heard.

## 4. Brain cramp

Sometimes people just forget. Remind them and give them another chance.

## 5. Disagreement with the goal

You may discover that your employee chose not to address the goal because he or she just plain disagreed with it. It doesn't happen often, but every now and then someone will say to you 'I'm not going to do that.' Now you have a challenge. Literally. In six words, your employee has thrown down a virtual gauntlet. He or she has chosen to become confrontational.

When this happens, your response must be black and white, with no room for your employee to wiggle out. Restate to the employee why the objective is important and tell the employee that, while you appreciate the concerns, you expect him or her to give a best effort at achieving the objective. The employee will probably try to argue with you and tell you why he or she thinks it is stupid. Whatever you do, don't argue back. You can acknowledge what the employee has said with an 'I hear you' or something similar, but the employee needs to recognize that you won't be backing down. Just like the referee in a football game, you might listen to a player's complaints, but you won't change the decision.

This is unquestionably the least comfortable scenario, and unfortunately many managers back down when faced with this kind of confrontation. The question you have to ask yourself is 'What are the consequences of backing down?' Not only do you send a message to the employee that you don't have a great deal of conviction in the goals you've set, but you also send a message to all of the other employees that they don't have to try if they don't want to either.

If the employee continues to exhibit this kind of behaviour over a period of time, you have no choice but to move to an employee dismissal strategy. Take a look at Chapter 12 to see how it's done.

Whichever strategy you end up using, positive, constructive or corrective, always remember that coaching is an exercise to educate, motivate and encourage the people who work for you. It's not about finding flaws in someone else's performance, and it's not about exercising power. It is a powerful, positive tool that can dramatically improve the performance levels of your team.

# 10

# The fine art of delegating

*So what are we going to do about it?*

'I swear to God, it seems to be the only thing that gives her enjoyment', the general manager of a large pharmaceutical company once told me of one of his employees. 'Whenever something has gone wrong, she comes into my office and tells me about it. Then she just stands there with this smirk on her face and watches me try to figure out what to do. Then, when I come up with a course of action, she stands there and picks holes in it. I'm convinced she lives to make me squirm.'

The fact is employees look to you, as their boss, for direction. That is, after all, your job. It's also true, however, that wherever possible employees will look to you to make their decisions for them, thus saving them from the risk of making an error in judgement. Given the opening, they might even let you do their work for them too. If you're really set on creating performance-challenged Employees from Hell, a great way to start is to avoid delegating.

If you've been in management for longer than a month, you've probably heard how important delegation is. The benefits are tremendous. Delegating tasks frees you up to do more important things, and it helps your employees to develop, it increases their sense of value and accomplishment, and it reduces the number of problems when you return from holiday.

Most of us are terrible at it. We don't have the patience or the skill. Most of us aren't willing to take the risk that comes with delegation, the risk of giving up control and trusting other people's decisions. We also fear the higher personal workload as we initially train and coach employees to do new things. Employees will struggle and fail as they progress through the learning curve – that's a given. But most of us are afraid to let that happen.

The fact is, though, you can't expect employees to have pride in the work that you're doing for them. You can't expect people to feel like valuable contributors when they aren't permitted to contribute anything valuable. You can't expect people to exude trust and respect for others when they don't feel trusted and respected themselves. Many performance issues with employees have less to do with the things you are asking them to do than with the things you aren't asking them to do.

A director of a large retail chain was once lamenting to me about a handful of his store managers who kept asking to be allocated more employee hours. 'Most of their stores are under-performing as it is', he said to me in frustration. 'Where do they think the money is going to come from to pay for all of these extra hours? I wish these people had a bit more business sense.'

I asked him why he thought they seemed so oblivious to the relationship between employee hours and store profitability.

'I don't know', he responded. 'It's not as though we haven't taught them how to read a profit and loss statement. This is pretty basic stuff!'

'So your managers are responsible for the profitability of their stores?' I asked.

'Yes', he responded. 'Well, indirectly, at least. I mean, aren't we all ultimately responsible for the profitability of the stores?'

And there was the problem. Store profitability was being used as the measuring stick for the performance of the stores, but the managers had no real control over how it was achieved.

I suggested to him that he take a handful of stores and charge the managers completely with their profitability. Have the managers create the budgets, and give them bonuses based on achieving or exceeding quarterly objectives. Monitor their activity on a monthly basis so that he could provide them with some guidance if they were making truly questionable decisions, but other than that let them make the decisions.

He tried it with six stores, including two with managers who'd been asking for more hours. The first two months were excruciating as the managers struggled with their newfound responsibility. Only one managed to hit his quarterly target. By the second quarter, though, all but one hit the target, and when the fourth quarter came around, the lucrative Christmas season, all but one exceeded their targets by wide margins.

The interesting part is that they all did it in different ways. One reduced hours to the bare minimum, while another increased staff to serve customers better. Another introduced a series of incentives and bonuses for hitting certain sales-per-hour targets. What they all had in common was a huge sense of pride in their accomplishments.

If the reason you haven't been delegating is a time-related issue (eg 'I don't have time to train someone'), you should conduct a little mathematical exercise. Estimate how many hours it would take to train and coach someone to be proficient at a specific task. Then estimate the amount of time you would normally spend on that task over the course of a year, two years or five years. Then simply subtract one number from the other. You might be shocked at the outcome.

If you aren't delegating because you don't think you have the right people, try the coaching process. If that doesn't work, refer to Chapter 12, 'Setting employees free'.

# The delegating process

Most people, when delegating, either 'delegate and drop' or micromanage. Neither approach is effective. Proper delegation is a gradual, nurturing process that eases both you and your employee into the change. If you want to become a better delegator, here are the seven steps you'll have to take.

## 1. Decide what is to be delegated

Begin by making a list of all the things you do on a given day. Which things are repetitive? Which consume most of your time? Which do you keep putting at the bottom of your 'to do' list? Now, with each of the elements, ask yourself 'What might I stand to gain by delegating this?' as well as 'What do I stand to lose if I delegate this?'

Not everything, of course, can or should be delegated. A CEO, for example, can't delegate board meetings (as much as he or she might like to), and a salesperson can't delegate a sales call. There are some things that require discretion and confidentiality. But the number of tasks that can be delegated is far greater than the number of those that can't. It's also a good idea not to delegate tasks that you find enjoyable. After all, those are the things that keep you coming to work every day.

## 2. Choose your delegatees

Once you have decided what to delegate, the next step is to decide whom to delegate to. The greatest challenge here is to avoid the 'give it to a busy person' trap. You probably have, as most managers do, one or two people whom you rely on. Your 'go to' people. They might be more confident, more eager or just a little more effective. As a result, they are the ones whom you turn to most often. The danger, of course, is that you run the risk of burning out a valuable employee and alienating the others.

As much as possible, try to delegate something to everyone. Delegate tasks only to people who have (or have potential for) proficiency in the area, and, when it comes to the less enjoyable jobs, don't heap them all on one person. Spread them around a bit.

## 3. Discuss the tasks with your employees

When you have a quiet moment, take your employee aside and ask the employee if he or she is willing to take on the additional responsibility. Explain what you are delegating, why you are delegating it, why you have chosen him or her for the job, and how both the employee and the company will benefit from the delegation. If your employee appears apprehensive about or uncomfortable with the job you are proposing, probe and listen carefully. Be prepared for the possibility that you may not have selected the right person after all.

## 4. Show your employees how to do the jobs

Instead of just throwing employees into their tasks, take the time to demonstrate to them exactly how you would like the jobs done. Be patient and continually confirm their under-standing.

## 5. Supervise your employees

For the first two or three times that employees do delegated tasks themselves, supervise them closely. This is your oppor-tunity to nit-pick a little and make sure that they are completely comfortable with the job.

## 6. Follow up instantly

For the first three times that an employee does the delegated task, you should follow up right away. Doing so allows you to correct any errors immediately, and it gives you the opportunity to provide your employee with plenty of positive reinforcement for a job well done.

## 7. Provide indirect, passive supervision

At this stage, your employee is ready to begin doing the del-egated job without direct supervision. You are now at the point where all you have to do is casually review the work. Once people have become comfortable with the things delegated to them, your goal shifts to teaching employees to solve their own problems.

My friend Tony Wackerman, manager for a large retailer, is without question the best delegator I've ever met. He excels at encouraging his employees to be problem solvers. I'll never forget sitting in his office one day in the late 1990s watching a steady parade of people coming in to see him for advice. (Tony is one of those rare individuals who actually has a real open-door policy.)

'We have a problem', the first person said. 'One of our stores doesn't have the proper signage for the sale that's starting tomorrow!'

'That is a problem', acknowledged Tony. 'So what are we going to do about it?'

The employee hesitated for a moment and then proposed a solution.

'Great', said Tony. 'Make it happen.'

Five minutes later another person dashed in. 'Tony,' she said breathlessly, 'one of our landlords has just told us that we can't open our temporary location tomorrow unless they have all of the signed lease documentation and our electrical layout. He said that he's going to be leaving his office in half an hour.'

'Oh dear', exclaimed Tony. 'What are we going to do about it?'

Again, after a brief hesitation, the employee outlined her plan.

And so it went. Ten or more times over a two-hour period. It was like watching a bizarre ping-pong game. An employee would come in and lob a ball into Tony's end, and Tony would quickly send it back. It was fun to watch and even more fun to watch the attitudes of the employees. Most were run off their feet – to say that the business ran lean was an understatement. But the sense of pride and accomplishment in what they did was palpable.

Here again are the seven steps to effective delegation:

1. Decide what is to be delegated.
2. Choose your delegatees.
3. Discuss the tasks with your employees.
4. Show your employees how to do the jobs.
5. Supervise your employees.
6. Follow up instantly.
7. Provide indirect, passive supervision.

# 11

# Carrots and sticks

*The key to motivating people is to push the right buttons in the right people, at the right times, for the right reasons.*

One of the tried-and-true strategies for boosting performance is through motivation, incentives and rewards. Sometimes the most unproductive and lackadaisical employee can become motivated with a little push in the proper direction. Motivation is often a misunderstood concept, however, and many people find themselves becoming frustrated with the lack of success their efforts achieve. The fact is not all people will be motivated by a good speech. And even those who are motivated by such a speech will respond to varying degrees depending on the situation.

In my volunteer work in young people's sports, helping coaches to develop skills for motivating their teams more effectively, I will, from time to time, volunteer to conduct the pre-game speech for a football team. I do this to illustrate the effect proper motivation can have on performance.

One instance was with a team in my area. They had been having a rough season to that point, with 10 losses and zero wins. After some discussion and planning with the coach, I conducted a 20-minute pre-game speech, and to everyone's delight, at the end of the game, the record stood at 10 losses and one win.

While it was an exciting moment, the point of the process was to demonstrate to the players that their previous losses had less to do with their own skill levels, or their coach's coaching ability, and more to do with their confidence and focus. And, while they still finished the season with a poor record, they at least knew that, when push came to shove, they were as good as any other team out there.

But the thing about motivation is that these pre-game speeches I give won't work a second time. Despite the energy and enthusiasm they generate, it is the players, not the speeches, who win the games. The speech gives them confidence and helps them to focus, but that is all. Its purpose is solely to break the inertia. From there, the strategy has to shift to building on the energy and enthusiasm, not reinventing it.

Motivation is a process, not a one-shot situation. And, as such, it requires proper planning. Different people are motivated by different things, and it is important to be aware of that before you begin. The key to motivating people is to push the right buttons in the right people, at the right times, for the right reasons.

There are two basic kinds of motivation: internal and external. Internally motivated people are those whose interests, beliefs, values and principles provide them with strong enough reasons to take action. They don't need a push – in fact, they are usually the ones doing the pushing. Externally motivated people are those who require an outside stimulus to take action. They need something or someone to give them a reason.

Nobody, of course, is completely internally motivated or completely externally motivated. The degree and type of motivation change depending on the task at hand. A friend of mine, for example, is a marathon runner. He is up at 5 am every morning, training diligently in order to prepare for the 26.4 gruelling miles. Nobody has to push him, and there's no big money for him at the end of the race. He does it purely out of a sense of pride and accomplishment. The only way his wife can get him to do the dishes, however, is by threatening to hide his golf clubs.

It would be wonderful if all employees were internally motivated to do a great job at work all the time, but that is rarely the case. Most managers find themselves with one or two employees who are difficult to motivate. To drive sales, productivity or other behaviours, therefore, we have to turn to an EM (external motivation) plan.

# EM drivers

Let's begin by examining what types of things motivate people. What are people's motivational drivers, and why is it that common motivational strategies sometimes don't work at all?

The two primary factors that contribute to the success of external motivation initiatives are the nature of the motivation and the manner in which it is delivered. The nature of the motivation can be either tangible or intangible. In other words, it can be a thing that has mass or substance, or it can be something symbolic or emotional. A tangible motivator might be the annual sales trip, the monthly bonus or the rise at the end of the year. An intangible motivator can be acknowledgement in the company newsletter, recognition as employee of the week, or praise from the boss for a job well done.

The manner in which the motivation is delivered can be either visible or discreet. Visible motivators are those that everyone can see. They are public recognition of a goal achieved or a job well done. They include public praise at the next staff meeting, a framed certificate or a badge. Discreet motivators are delivered quietly and personally, often with other people never knowing about them. They range from a telephone call at home from the boss to an unadvertised day off with pay.

It's important to be aware of these distinctions because they can play a significant role in the success of your external motivation plan. I first became aware of these distinctions when I was running a small chain of toy shops. I was becoming increasingly frustrated with my attempts to incentivize employees. If I had a contest, some would jump in with both feet, while others would duck their heads and ignore it entirely. When I tried a bonus plan to encourage people to help the shop hit its targets, some people rallied and worked incredibly hard, while others appeared not to care at all. The curious thing was that it never seemed to be the same people who were motivated each time.

When the nature and delivery of motivation are combined, you get a matrix that looks like the one in Figure 11.1. Each quadrant is a motivational driver. To better identify them, I've named them after the classic four elements: earth, fire, water and wind.

Virtually everyone has either one dominant motivational driver and one secondary motivational driver or two equally dominant motivational drivers. In general terms, here is how they are differentiated.

## Earth (visible/tangible)

Earth is motivated by things that are tangible and delivered in a highly visible format, for example:

- a jacket with the company's logo;
- a publicly announced promotion;
- publicly awarded prizes;
- greater authority or responsibility;
- a preferred parking place; or
- business cards.

|  | Tangible | Intangible |
|---|---|---|
| Visible | EARTH | FIRE |
| Discreet | WATER | WIND |

**Figure 11.1** Matrix of motivational drivers

Although it is hard to tell through the bragging, Earth types are somewhat insecure with their abilities and accomplishments. It is very important to them that they are recognized for their efforts and that everyone is aware of the recognition – particularly the boss.

## Fire (visible/intangible)

Fire types are motivated by highly visible recognition that comes more from the heart than the wallet. Being employee of the week, appearing in the company's newsletter or being held up as a role model at the quarterly conference appeals to them. They are proud of doing the job they are paid to do, and, while they crave the recognition, they don't necessarily feel the need for additional compensation. Other examples of Fire motivators include:

- invitations to lead or be involved in high-profile projects;
- award pins and badges;
- a plaque recognizing accomplishments or certification; and
- invitations to planning meetings and business trips.

## Water (discreet/tangible)

Water types are motivated by things that are tangible, but are uncomfortable being in the spotlight. They are often concerned that others will become jealous or judgemental. They will work hard for bonuses and commissions, where the compensation is usually privately concluded, but will shy away from excelling in contests and competitions. Other Water motivators include:

- time off with pay (eg afternoons for golf);
- preferred shifts;
- coffee/lunch paid for by the boss; and

▓ theatre tickets quietly handed out or put in with the pay slip.

## Wind (discreet/intangible)

Wind types actively avoid any obvious motivational device. While they respond extremely well to expressions of appreciation or recognition, they do not like to feel manipulated. They perceive themselves as somewhat above such things. You will often find that the Employees from Hell you are having the hardest time motivating have Wind as their primary driver. Motivation for Wind must appear spontaneous and genuine. Wind motivators include:

▓ private recognition;
▓ an invitation to planning meetings;
▓ a thank-you phone call at home;
▓ a pat on the back or a 'Good job!';
▓ a letter of recommendation; and
▓ an invitation to a buying/training trip.

Over the years, as my company has taken groups of people through analyses to determine their drivers, we have noticed some broad generalities. Commissioned salespeople, for example, have a tendency to fall into the more tangible Earth and Water categories. Engineers and other people in the sciences tend to fall into the more discreet Water and Wind categories. Entrepreneurs and senior managers lean heavily toward the more visible Earth and Fire categories. Having said all this, we have also discovered that it is impossible to predict someone's motivational drivers based solely on position or occupation. Motivation is a very personal thing.

When you consider how different each motivational driver is, it's easy to understand why it is virtually impossible for company-wide EM programmes to stimulate every employee. It's also easy to see how, if you implement the wrong plan, it can even have an adverse effect with the performance-challenged

Employee from Hell. The employee who falls into the Wind category may be scornful of an Earth-focused incentive. The employee in the Fire category may be disappointed with the less visible Water approach.

One of the biggest reasons that EM programmes are not as effective as they could be is that we don't take the time to think them through. We think 'Last year we ran the Trip to Florida reward programme, and it seemed to work – let's try it again this year', 'We tried that "dinner with the boss" thing last year, and it was a flop – I'm never doing that again' or 'XYZ company is using this promotion, and it's really working well for them – I think we should try it.' Before introducing an EM plan, you need to take a close look at which employees you are targeting. Recognize that you won't be able to reach everyone, and decide which employees you do want to reach. Only after you've determined this can you make an appropriate decision on how you are going to reach them.

Once you know whom you want to reach, and have assessed which categories they fall into, the next step is to determine the approach to take. There are three fundamental EM strategies: incentives, inducements and rewards.

## Incentives

An incentive is an external motivator that is something positive for people to work toward. In other words, a carrot. Incentives are announced ahead of time and are attached to concrete, measurable targets. For example, a programme in which everyone achieving his or her budget receives £50 is an incentive plan. An incentive is used to encourage people to hit specific sales targets, to achieve certain scores on mystery shopping or customer satisfaction reports, to achieve certain closing ratios, to complete projects within budget or time parameters, and so on. Incentives are appropriate for people motivated by tangible things – Earth and Water.

## Inducements

While an incentive is tied to an end result, an inducement is a motivator tied to the means to that end. It is compensation for specific action. For example, a salesperson may receive a £2 commission for each one of a specific product sold, or a call centre employee may get a £5 bonus for every difficult customer not escalated to the supervisor. Inducements are always tangible, and typically financial, although substitutes such as film passes or gift tokens can also be used.

Inducement and incentive strategies can be run at the same time. You can, for instance, run an incentive programme that gives everyone in the department a free lunch if the department is under all of its expense budgets for the month. At the same time, you can give out free film passes every time someone improves a process to help achieve that goal. The two work together towards the same end. As with incentive strategies, inducements are tangible motivators and appeal to Earth and Water.

## Rewards

A reward is an acknowledgment of a job well done. The difference between a reward and an incentive or inducement is that, while people appreciate the recognition, it is not necessarily the motivation to do the job. Rewards are given after the fact, for a specific accomplishment, and are not always announced ahead of time. Rewards are effective in boosting team or individual morale, expressing thanks, encouraging future successes, creating pride in the workplace and so on.

Rewards can be visible, such as recognition in the company newsletter, or discreet, such as quietly giving employees some extra time off at the end of the day. But, because a reward is not necessarily either concrete or announced ahead of time, it appeals more to Fire and Wind – people attracted to intangible motivators.

A well-planned and well-executed EM plan can have a significant impact on both productivity and morale. A poorly planned or executed one can backfire and cause headaches for everyone. One company, for example, used to give its employees a turkey every year at Christmas to thank them for their roles in the company's profitability. For some 15 years in a row, employees never had to worry about their Christmas turkey. In 1991, the deep recession caused the company to lose money for the first time in its history, and come Christmastime there was not a turkey in sight. The union put in a grievance – and won – citing that the turkey was now part of the expected employee compensation package. The turkey had ceased to become a reward.

To reiterate the point I made at the beginning of this chapter, an external motivator is effective only when it pushes the right buttons in the right people, at the right times, for the right reasons. If you are experiencing performance challenges with Employees from Hell who are feeling unnoticed or underappreciated, a sustained and well-thought-out EM plan can have a tremendous impact. Tied with a positive management style and a positive work environment, it can dramatically lift a group's energy and productivity.

# 12

# Setting employees free

*If you have to swallow a frog, it's a good idea if you don't stare at it too long.*

You've tried everything. The working environment is wonderful, you're wonderful, you've set performance standards, you've coached and you've attempted to motivate. Yet you still have that Employee from Hell driving you mad. It might be time for the end game. The F-bomb.

Back in the olden days, we called it 'firing'. Then, somewhere in the mid-1980s, some Enlightened People decided that the term 'being fired' was hurting the feelings of the firees and began to come up with a myriad of gentler terms. These days employers dehire, have a permanent lay-off, deplace, jettison, downsize, move on, put them off work, rightsize, surplus and trim people, but no one gets fired any more. Somehow these words are supposed to soften the blow of getting sacked. Right. As a flippant commentary on this trend, our company began, in our management skills workshops, to refer to firing people as 'setting employees free'.

Knowing how and when to fire an employee is a tremendously valuable skill. It's also a very necessary skill. Done properly, it can have an immediate and wide-ranging positive effect on an organization. Done poorly, it can cause a myriad of headaches. Not done at all, you might be haunted in a hundred different ways.

I'll never forget the first person I had to fire. She was an account executive I had inherited when I joined the company. She had a knack of saying inappropriate things at inappropriate times, and, despite an inordinate amount of coaching, she was completely unable to connect with either clients or colleagues. She was also unable to meet any deadlines set for her, and as a result she was largely ineffective at her job. I found myself constantly covering for her failures and scrambling to fix her work.

I delayed the decision for almost three months. I kept hoping that she would magically begin to improve. She didn't, of course, and it wasn't until one of my colleagues said to me 'When are you going to stop whining about her and just do something?' that I finally took action.

The positive changes began almost immediately. Clients were more responsive, there was less tension in the office and I was sleeping better. Three other employees came to me and confided how good a decision they thought I'd made. The change was even good for the employee I fired. She ended up moving into a career that she found much more satisfying. The lesson I learnt that day is that, when you know what you have to do – just do it.

Bosses and managers have all kinds of strategies for trying to avoid firing employees. Some try to ignore them, as I did, and hope things will get better. Some begin to give them increasingly more disagreeable work in the hope that they will start looking for another job. Some transfer them to a different department. Some demote them in the hope that they'll see the writing on the wall and quit.

My brother-in-law, Tim, is a senior manager with a large software company. Here is the story he told of inheriting someone who'd recently been demoted:

> He was originally the sales manager but could not motivate or organize the sales group. He was demoted to sales rep. And then I was hired. He was bright and very knowledgeable. He could deal with the most arcane discussion about what is a very large and very complex

software package. But he could not develop or articulate a simple sales strategy. His software demonstrations were hideous affairs where he jumped all over the map, where there was absolutely no flow and no cohesion to the demo.

After repeated discussions about these problems and increasingly dire warnings, he finally confessed that he had attention deficit disorder. His psychiatrist had put him on medication the previous month, and everything was going to be OK. Things did not improve. There was no alternative position within the company, and there was no one in the organization who wanted him anyway. I finally had to fire him.

Think of what might have happened had this employee just been set free in the first place. The company would probably have gained more business, Tim wouldn't have inherited a challenge that consumed his valuable time, and the employee wouldn't have had to deal with the stress and embarrassment of being demoted before his peers – and then fired.

There are four fundamental steps to setting employees free.

# 1. Get a second opinion

Before you begin the process, confidentially outline your thoughts to your boss or a peer you trust. Get this person's thoughts. Listen to this person. If he or she agrees that your course of action is the right one, continue to the next stage. If he or she doesn't agree with your course of action, you may ultimately still want to continue to the next stage, but at least you'll have questioned your own perspective.

# 2. Cover your bases

Check any protocols or procedures that your company may have for dismissing employees. If you have an HR department, ask someone there for input. If neither option is available to you, be fully aware of the labour laws and follow the proper process. As a minimum, you will want to make sure that you have given your employee at least one verbal warning and one written warning prior to taking dismissal action. Ensure that you are offering at least the minimum compensation package required by law. In today's highly litigious atmosphere, you want to make sure that you have left nothing to chance.

# 3. Set a decision date

Pick a date in the near future – no longer than 10 days. Mark it on your calendar so that you don't forget. Unless you see some miraculous or dramatic improvement, that is the day you will break the news.

# 4. Break the news

A former franchisee of mine had a saying: 'If you have to swallow a frog, it's a good idea if you don't stare at it too long.' When you're meeting with your employee, don't beat about the bush. Get straight to the point. The best way to begin is 'John, I'm afraid we're going to have to let you go.' Pause for a moment to let your employee respond. Whatever you do, don't enter into an argument with the employee, and don't get into a philosophical discussion about the wisdom of your decision. Simply outline the details.

Following are some examples of how the employee might respond and appropriate ways for you to react:

> John: But I've been getting better! I'm really trying!
> Boss: Unfortunately, your performance is still below par. Here is a copy of your severance package.
> John: You can't fire me – I have a family to look after!
> Boss: I'm sorry, John. I understand your predicament. Here is a copy of your severance package.
> John: I knew this was coming! You've never liked me. This is completely unfair. You're going to regret this!
> Boss: Maybe so. Here is a copy of your severance package.

You don't have to be quite that abrupt, of course, but it is important that you try to avoid discussions that prolong the discomfort for either you or your employee.

I don't think I've ever met anyone who actually enjoys firing people. It is sometimes, however, one of those necessary evils. If you've tried everything – set immutable performance standards, and tried coaching and motivating – and the employee's performance hasn't improved, there becomes little choice. It may help to realize that, by the time you've reached this point, your employee is probably as unsatisfied as you are. Nobody, after all, wants to be a failure, or unproductive, or unsatisfied with what he or she does. One reason our tongue-in-cheek term 'setting employees free' actually caught on is that, in many respects, this is exactly what you are doing. Not only are you giving yourself, your team and your company an opportunity for a stronger, more productive atmosphere, but you are also giving the employee an opportunity to find a new job in which he or she might excel. The employee may be losing the job, but with any luck he or she won't lose the lesson.

Here again are the four basic steps to setting employees free:

1.  Get a second opinion.
2.  Cover your bases.
3.  Set a decision date.
4.  Break the news.

# 13

# Poison in the pool and curious quirks

*There seems to be an incalculable number of weird and wonderful behaviours that you can run into as a manager.*

If the only Employees from Hell you had to deal with were people simply not performing up to standard, life wouldn't really be so bad. Using the strategies and concepts outlined in the previous chapters can help you with most of them. Unfortunately, employees can sometimes present an entirely different type of challenge. Sometimes we find ourselves having to deal with… interesting… and sometimes strange personalities.

There seems to be an incalculable number of weird and wonderful behaviours that you can run into as a manager. Because they are so diverse, and at times so extreme, it would be impossible to develop an all-encompassing strategy for dealing with them. In this chapter, we'll take a look at a cross-section of some of the more prevalent and detrimental personality-challenged Employees from Hell and at some specific techniques for dealing with them.

To help define these Employees from Hell better, I have divided them into two categories: Poison in the Pool (employees whose behaviour creates a significant negative impact on the entire team) and Curious Quirks (employees whose counter-productive or just plain annoying behaviour primarily affects their own performance or their relationships with you).

# Poison in the pool

## The Whiner

Some people, it seems, simply aren't happy unless they're unhappy. No matter what's going on, no matter how well things are going, they'll find something to complain about. They get great satisfaction from putting clouds on to silver linings. We've all seen these people. When business is quiet, they whine because they're bored. When things get busy, they whine because they're overwhelmed. They have sore backs, bad bosses, bad colleagues, rude customers and bunions. Left unchecked, these people can slowly but surely drag down the entire team – and you with it. They can put a damper on any of your attempts to motivate the team, and you don't dare greet them by saying 'Hello, how are you?' because they'll probably tell you, and it won't be pleasant.

Whining, or chronic complaining, is a type of patterned behaviour. Most often the people who behave this way in your business environment behave the same way in their social environments. And the interesting thing is that most of these people don't realize they're whining to the extent they are, and typically they're unaware of the impact they're having on the team.

To deal with Whiners, and it's very important that you do deal with them, you have to begin by separating the behaviour from the person. Most people can accept, albeit grudgingly, that from time to time they exhibit behaviour that is inappropriate. Nobody, however, likes to think of him- or herself as a bad person. Saying 'You are a negative influence on the rest of the team' or labelling somebody a 'whiner' will be completely ineffective, with the net result that you have just given the person something else to whine about.

The other challenge is that, because it is patterned behaviour – behaviour exhibited on a consistent basis – it won't be corrected overnight. It has been programmed into the person for years – sometimes a lifetime – and the deprogramming process is neither easy nor quick. The good news is that most Whiners can be turned around, but it does require diligence and patience on your part.

The first thing you need to do is get the person alone – either in your office or in the local coffee shop. Introduce the subject by using a variation of the good stuff–bad stuff–good stuff format.

## Good stuff

Begin by outlining what you consider to be the person's strengths and contributions to the company. Something like 'Jane, I think you know what it is that you bring to this company. You have tremendous experience, and you always get the job done.'

## Bad stuff

Again, no 'buts', 'howevers' or 'althoughs'. Keep it positive. The best way to start with the corrective part is by saying 'There's something I need you to do for me. I don't think you've noticed it, but a lot of times the things that you say are, well, kind of negative. And my concern is that people may begin to think of you as a bit of a whiner. Now, I'm sure that's not a perception that you'd like to have, and it certainly isn't some-thing that I want, because that kind of negative energy can really start to bring down the team. Can I get you to, over the next little while, maybe be a little more conscious of the things you say and the way you say them? I think it would be in everyone's best interests.'

## Good stuff

Make sure you let the person know it isn't a condemnation of him or her as much as an observation on behaviour. You need the person to believe that you don't think of him or her as a bad person and that you believe the person is capable of improving. For example, you might say 'I wouldn't be telling you this if you weren't such an important member of this team. I really need your help on this.'

## Commitment

Finish off the conversation with a simple commitment question, such as 'Can I count on you?' or 'Will you give it a try?'

Be prepared for the employee to become a little defensive. If that happens, tell the employee about some specific instances so that he or she understands what you're talking about. Make sure that the employee knows these are examples only and that, if it was just something happening now and then, you wouldn't even have bothered to bring it up.

The next step requires a little diligence on your part. It is critical that you interrupt the pattern now every time you see it. So, if you happen to be walking by the employee's desk while he or she's hanging up the phone, for example, and you hear the employee say 'Oh, it's that stupid customer of ours, old Mr Smith, calling in to complain again', make a point of reacting to it. You don't have to make a big scene – just tap the employee on the shoulder and look at him or her with raised eyebrows and a 'Remember what we talked about?' kind of look. The employee probably won't respond well to this and might get a little defensive. But once you've done it a dozen times or so, you'll find that the employee will become much more aware of his or her behaviour patterns, and will be whining less frequently.

## The Gossip

The office environment is rather like that in a small town. There are always a few people intent on knowing what everybody else is doing and on sharing that information with others. The Gossip knows who's dating whom, who has a drinking problem, who's had a promotion and who's in trouble. The sad truth is that, if companies could figure out how to spread positive and relevant information as effectively as the Gossip can communicate negative and irrelevant information, they would all be flourishing.

Unfortunately, the information people get from Gossips is rarely completely accurate and is generally tainted by the Gossips' opinions. The trap for many bosses is that Gossips are often also their source of information. They are the ones to whom a boss might turn to get the 'pulse' of the company. They are the people who will volunteer opinions that they claim are really the opinions of those in the office who are uncomfortable expressing themselves. If Gossips have their own agendas, it's easy for a boss to take actions and make decisions that can be counterproductive at best.

If you have a Gossip, and your other employees believe that the Gossip has your ear, your ability to communicate with the team is compromised considerably. I once experienced first-hand the negative impact of the Gossip on open and honest communications while conducting a series of focus groups as part of a client needs analysis. One of the groups was noticeably hesitant to share information and far less candid in its comments and opinions. No matter what tactic I took, I couldn't help but get the feeling I wasn't getting the whole story. After the session was over, one of the participants approached me and asked if I'd noticed this behaviour. I told him I had, and he explained why it had happened. 'One of the people in the room,' he explained, 'is the manager's pet. And nothing ever happens around here that the manager doesn't find out about. He's a nice guy and all, but nobody really trusts him very much.'

Gossips are virtually impossible to stop, short of just firing them. But they can be controlled. They're hard to stop because they're typically fairly outgoing people by nature. They like to know things and are unhappy when they don't know things. They don't perceive themselves as busybodies or meddlers. They do, however, perceive themselves as being in the proverbial loop.

The best way to deal with Gossips is not to fight them but to enlist them and redirect them. Begin by acknowledging that they have a good handle on everything that is going on, and tell them that you need their help. Tell them that you've noticed some of the rumours going around the workplace that, in the long run, may hurt the team. (Don't mention the fact that it was probably they who started them in the first place.) Ask them if they will take on the role as de facto guardians of company morale. If they hear anyone say something negative about or debilitating to the company, their role will be to try to spin it into a positive.

You then have to explain to them that, in order to be effective in their role, they will need to earn and retain the confidence of their colleagues. Hence, they will have to refrain from providing you with the kind of input that they have in the past. Tell them that, as much as you appreciate their information and updates, their role as 'morale officer' will have a far greater positive impact on the company.

This approach allows you to use the Gossip's strength to the company's advantage while setting the stage for greater trust in the workplace. The compromise in using this strategy is that you're losing a source of information. Given the potentially questionable nature of the information, however, that's not necessarily a bad thing.

## Jealous Joe

I remember sitting in a pub once with a group of colleagues when one announced that she had just received a promotion. Drinks were raised all around as we all scrambled to congratulate her. She was a bright and likeable person, and we were all thrilled for her. Well, almost all of us.

After she left, one of my colleagues, I'll call him Joe, began seething. 'I can't believe she got the promotion!' he exclaimed angrily. 'I've been here for five years. If there's anyone who deserves a promotion, it's me!'

The outburst didn't really surprise anyone much. Joe frequently went crazy whenever somebody got something he didn't have. When I had received new office furniture a month before, he had marched straight into his boss's office to demand why he hadn't got new office furniture. When one of our colleagues was invited to speak at a function, Joe made a huge fuss about how he should be speaking at functions. He just couldn't stand the idea of somebody else being successful.

There are many people like Joe who measure their self-worth based not on their own accomplishments but on how well they are doing in comparison to those around them. It's a 'keep up with the Joneses' mentality. These people tend to be highly judgemental of others' accomplishments and are typically very vocal in their thoughts. Their inward focus completely prevents them from celebrating team goals and the achievements of others, and they can be a heavy drain on a group's positive momentum.

Unfortunately, it is unlikely that you can change the way Jealous Joes think. At some level, they will always compare themselves to others and see success as a relative thing. But you can try to control their impact on the rest of the team.

Your best bet with Jealous Joes is to be direct with them and consistent in your actions. Begin by meeting with the employee alone. Your meeting should be positive, and, as always, you should begin by letting the employee know how valuable he or she is to you and the company. When you present the challenge to the employee, you should be direct without being accusatory. Relate to the employee two or three instances in which his or her jealousy surfaced, and explain that the decisions you make are based on individual assessments, needs and requirements. Explain how the employee's actions have affected the team and why it is important that he or she makes an effort not to damage the team's morale. Let the employee know that he or she can always come to you with anything perceived to be an injustice, but be clear that you will not discuss other people's situations with the employee.

Whatever you do, don't allow yourself to fall into an argument with the employee, and absolutely don't let the employee drag you into a discussion about his or her value in comparison to somebody else's. You will have to be both consistent and diligent in your approach, because the employee won't be able to stop his or her behaviour easily. The employee's brain tells him or her there has been an injustice, and it may always do so. Your strategy is to try to keep the employee quiet.

## Mr Sarcastic

When I was a child, my parents used to drill into my head that, 'If you can't say anything nice about someone, don't say anything at all.' Some people never understood that message. I'm convinced that every workplace has a Mr Sarcastic. Mr Sarcastic rarely takes the forefront, and rarely contributes anything positive, preferring instead to sit in the background making snide remarks about the things everyone else is doing.

Sarcasm, when it is chronic, is a defence mechanism. 'As long as I sit in the judgement seat, I am less likely to be judged myself' is the underlying thought. Few people want to judge Mr Sarcastic harshly for fear that Mr Sarcastic might turn on them. And make no mistake about it, although cloaked in the guise of humour, sarcasm can be more devastating than outright condemnation when directed at a specific person or company.

On its own, sarcasm is a wonderful form of humour. It gets people to look at things from different perspectives, and it can serve as a great release during tense situations. It starts to become harmful, however, when it is persistent or directed. Its impact on the team can be so strong that people become literally paralysed for fear that any action they take will be made fun of.

This is one of the few situations with an Employee from Hell that can't be effectively dealt with directly. If you were to call the employee into your office to talk, he or she would simply turn it around and use it against you. 'I got the big talk today', the employee might say later to colleagues. 'Apparently, I'm too sarcastic. As though there's nothing to be sarcastic about around here...'

There is only one way that I know of to deal with such an employee effectively, and that is to use your position power to beat the employee at his or her own game. It's not pretty, but it works. Every time you hear the employee make a sarcastic remark, come back with a sarcastic remark of your own that tells the employee his or her behaviour is not acceptable. Here are a few comebacks that you can try:

- 'Slow day in the positive attitude department today, John?'
- 'If only you could use that biting wit for goodness and niceness, instead of evil.'
- 'Ah, thank you, John, for putting that cloud on our silver lining.'
- 'Nothing like a little sarcasm in the morning to motivate the team, right, John?'
- 'I think the phrase is "Early to bed, early to rise", not "Surly to bed, surly to rise".'
- 'Thank you for that productive contribution, John.'
- 'Don't be yourself, John, be nice.'

Remember that such employees are using sarcasm, at least in part, as a defence mechanism. They are trying to avoid being judged. The effect of 'reverse sarcasm' is that, every time they make a sarcastic remark, you are judging them. Two things will happen. The first is that there's a good chance they will quickly begin to tone down their behaviour to avoid criticism from their boss. The second is that the other employees, in hearing your responses, get the message that such behaviour is not acceptable, which effectively begins to remove any power the sarcastic comments may have.

## Snake in the Grass

Every now and then you run into employees who want to get ahead and decide to use your head as one of their stepping stones. Although they are often very friendly to your face, behind your back – to their colleagues, your peers and your superiors – they take shots at everything from your management style to your decision-making abilities.

They believe that they are considerably cleverer than you are, and they are trying hard to convince everyone else of this. Their approach is typically a passive–aggressive one. They will rarely, if ever, come out and challenge you, but they will try to raise questions. They'll say things to other employees like 'Well, I don't really know why Bob has decided to do it this way, but I'm just a company person and I do what I'm told.' Or they'll suggest hidden agendas in the things that you do: 'Of course that's the reason he wants people to believe...' They might try subtly to discredit you with your boss by saying, for instance, 'I suppose Bob never got around to telling us that' or 'I'm sure that Bob means well, but...' They will cast doubt on your leadership at every opportunity.

Left unchecked, Snakes in the Grass can undermine your every effort and potentially your career. The best way to deal with them is an approach that they will be the least comfortable with – a direct approach. Begin by telling the employee that you want a meeting. Pick a specific date, time and place a few days ahead to give the employee some time to ponder what you're going to talk to him or her about.

When the meeting starts, confront the employee immediately by saying something like 'Janet, you seem to be having a problem with me', and let the statement hang in the air to see how the employee responds. In all likelihood, the employee will reply with something like 'What do you mean?' Your goal at this point is to let the employee know, without directly threatening him or her, that you are aware of what he or she's been doing and that you won't tolerate it in the future.

To accomplish this goal, you employ a passive–aggressive tactic of your own. Begin by identifying to the employee two or three comments that you know he or she's made. Tell the employee that, if it were just one comment, you could overlook it as a one-off thing and that, if it were just two comments, you could write them off as coincidence. But, because of the frequency, it's apparent that there's something else behind them. The language you use in the last part is important because you need to trigger a response. Here are some examples:

- 'Clearly, you are trying to send me a message.'
- 'You obviously have a reason for doing this.'
- 'Clearly, something is motivating you to say these things.'

Follow your last statement with silence to give the employee time to answer. The response will take one of two forms. Either the employee will tell you what is actually on his or her mind, or, as is vastly more likely, the employee will claim that the comments were made in all innocence and that you have completely misread them. Rather than begin an argument by challenging the denial, accept it without apology and spell out your position and why the employee's behaviour is destructive. Here's an example of how you can present it:

> Janet, for the moment I'm willing to give you the benefit of the doubt as to why you're saying these things. But you have to recognize the impact that they have on the team, not to mention the impact they can have on me. I would appreciate it if you would be more careful of the way you say things in the future.

Regardless of the real reasons behind the employee's sniping, you've made it clear that it isn't acceptable, and you've alluded to the fact that you will be monitoring the employee's behaviour. It's not a particularly fun strategy to execute, but it is effective, and it is definitely more pleasant than the consequences of allowing the sniping to continue.

## Napoleon Blown-apart

Have you ever met one of those people who always seem to be right on the edge of losing it? When things aren't going exactly as planned, or people aren't doing things just so, they get wound up more tightly than an Egyptian mummy. Explosive employees are typically hard workers, play by the rules and are generally polite and respectful to colleagues. They just don't handle stressful situations well. When those situations occur, they raise the anxiety levels of everyone around them.

I once had an explosive colleague who worked in the office beside me. At least once a week, the frustrated shouting and cursing would literally drown out any conversation I might have been engaged in. Once a month or so, I would be jolted out of my seat by the sound of a telephone or other office parapher-nalia being hurtled against our mutual wall. Having said this, on the projects on which we worked together, we got along famously – but I still found myself walking on eggshells whenever we hit a glitch.

I learnt the secret for dealing with him from another colleague. Just as they would begin a project, he'd turn to our explosive colleague and say 'Frank, I don't want to see any of that famous temper of yours!' Frank would smile at him, but my colleague would persist. 'No, I want you to understand – if you can't control it, let me know now, and I'll find someone else to work with.' He never had a problem with Frank.

The greatest challenge for such people is that they have never learnt the skills for managing their emotional state. They have never had to – most people simply back away from them when they are angry and don't want to run the risk of annoying them again by bringing it up later. They have also learnt that the occasional outburst can work to their advantage because fewer people have the courage to question their work or decisions.

As a manager, your best strategy for dealing with such an employee is very similar to the way my colleague dealt with Frank. During a quiet moment, let the employee know that you won't permit that behaviour with you or anyone else on the team. You don't have to explain why; you simply have to be direct and clear. The next time the employee blows – and he or she will – wait until the employee has settled down, and then ask him or her for a meeting. Let the employee know that you're disappointed with him or her. Reiterate your expectations, and advise the employee that there will be consequences the next time it happens. And when it happens again – which it will – apply those consequences.

It's important that you don't avoid or ignore this type of Employee from Hell. By not doing anything, you give such employees tacit permission to continue with their behaviour, and other employees will begin to question your judgement and your leadership abilities.

## The Bully

Bullies come across as supremely confident. They are completely self-focused, and their own needs are inevitably a priority. They give no consideration to other people. To get their way, they won't hesitate to threaten, badger, browbeat, embarrass or intimidate other people. Those people include their subordinates, peers, colleagues, suppliers, customers and even you. They can raise the tension level in a room just by being there. This is the same type of person who pushed people around in the playground, and who lights up a cigarette in a lift and drives too closely on the motorway.

Bullies operate on the principle that most people will back away from confrontation. So they create confrontation, or the threat of confrontation, at every opportunity. Having a bully as a member of the team can have a catastrophic effect on productivity and the general office environment. The dilemma with having bullies among your employees, however, is that despite their unpleasant natures they almost always achieve their goals.

'I'm not crazy about the way she goes about things,' the GM of a large retail chain once said about one of his district sales managers, 'but she certainly gets things done.' He was right, and it was hard to argue with him. It wasn't a year after that conversation, however, that the unhappy people in that DSM's territory successfully spearheaded a movement to unionize the employees.

The issue with bullies is that you have to weigh their effectiveness, their productivity, against the productivity of the team as a whole. If you have 10 employees, and the Bully's negative behaviour reduces the performance of the other nine by just 10 per cent, the Bully would literally have to be twice as productive as any of them to make his or her behaviour acceptable.

The best way to deal with bullies is to redefine to them how their performance will be measured. Remembering that they are goal driven and motivated by self-interest, you have to try to change their perception of what is in their best interests. If elements of teamwork and attitude aren't already included in the criteria for the Bully's regular performance reviews, add them to the mix. If they're already included in the criteria, reweight them so that they become more significant factors. Once you've done this, sit down, tell the Bully what you have done and explain why.

Tell the Bully that, while you are not unhappy with the results that he or she is achieving, you have concerns about the methods. Make sure that you have specific examples to give. Tell the Bully that you are responsible for the effectiveness of the performance of the team as a whole and that you can't permit behaviour that jeopardizes that.

It is important that, prior to your meeting with the Bully, you are exceptionally well prepared. Remember that the Bully's modus operandi is confrontation, and he or she probably won't be afraid to try to confront or intimidate you as well. If the Bully does become confrontational, don't argue – but do stand your ground. You may find, in fact, that any bullying tactics the Bully uses during the meeting you can use to your advantage. Here are some examples of how you might handle it.

## Example 1

*Bully: Look, if you don't like the way I deal with things, I'm sure that I can find a position somewhere at the competition.*
*You: Now you see, Sally, that's exactly the kind of behaviour I was talking about. If you feel that that behaviour will be acceptable to the competition, and you feel that you would like to leave and work for them, that's your choice, and I can't stop you. But using it as a threat is inappropriate.*

## Example 2

*Bully: So what am I hearing you saying? You don't care how good a job I do, and you just want me to be nice to people? I mean, if you want me to be nice, and ineffective, I can do that, but I don't see how that's going to work to the benefit of this company.*
You: Now you see, Sally, that's exactly the kind of behaviour I was talking about. I didn't suggest that, and putting those words in my mouth is unproductive. Now, if you don't know how to be productive as a positive member of a team, we can arrange for training to help you develop those skill sets. If what you are saying is that you are just unwilling to make the effort, however, that's a different story altogether.

## Example 3

*Bully: I can't believe this! I'm the only one hitting all of the targets all the time. I'm the only one getting anything done around here. And you're telling me that I'm the problem? It would take you two people to replace me!*
You: Now you see, Sally, that's exactly the kind of behaviour I was talking about. There are 12 people in this department, and you are focused exclusively on you. That's not the way a team functions.

Don't let the Bully's productivity levels dissuade you from moving to a dismissal strategy if you believe it's in the company's best interests. You may be surprised at how well the rest of the team responds when this negative influence is taken out of the mix.

As a final note about dealing with Bullies, make sure that at all times your i's are dotted and your t's are crossed. If you have to move towards a dismissal strategy, you don't want to be remotely vulnerable to wrongful dismissal litigation.

# Curious Quirks

Not all Employees from Hell, of course, have the same direct and dramatic impact on the rest of the team as those outlined in Poison in the Pool. There are many others who range from simply unpleasant to have around to just plain weird. I call them Curious Quirks. And, while they aren't quite as destructive as Poison in the Pool types, their behaviour can still be a distraction and negatively affect the productivity of themselves and those around them. Following are a few examples of Curious Quirks and some strategies for dealing with them.

## Sunshine up the Shorts (Mr Everything)

As a manager, you can't help but love employees who are always positive. And, if every employee were as willing and eager to take on new responsibilities as Mr Everything, our lives would all be greatly simplified. These employees, however, pose a different kind of problem. They are the people who volunteer for everything. No matter what is on their plate, they will always want to take on more. It's not just a matter of their not being able to say no (which they can't); they actively seek out a continually increasing workload. The net effect is that they often find themselves unable to meet the deadline on anything.

Characteristically, they have a great deal of insecurity about their value and contribution to the company. Taking on more and more tasks is their way of trying to convince you, and themselves, that they are valuable – perhaps indispensable – members of the team. They are loyal to the company and feel as though they have a personal stake in its success.

The last thing you want to do is quell their eagerness or positive energy. What they need more than anything is reassurance about the importance of the work they are currently involved with. There are two things that you have to do. First, regularly remind them of the importance of their current projects and goals and how much you appreciate the job they are doing on them. Second, when they offer to take on new projects that you think might overwhelm them, you have to restate that message and let them know how much you appreciate their eagerness and enthusiasm. Say something like 'John, I really appreciate your offer, and I really think you could do a good job on it. But right now I really need your expertise on the projects you're working on. They are very important to the company, and I don't want anything to stand in the way of them being complete successes.' In a brief statement like this, you can indicate that you appreciate the employee's willingness, respect his or her abilities and value his or her work.

## Mr Impossible

The opposite of Mr Everything is Mr Impossible. If you ever want to develop a master list of why a task or project can't be done, just talk to Mr Impossible. Whether it is insufficient human resources, shortage of time, lack of funding, inadequate knowledge or whatever, such employees will try to dissuade you from having them do anything different from, or in addition to, what they are already doing.

Although their reluctance is often perceived as laziness, that is rarely the real issue. Often it is simply insecurity. Some people just don't handle change well. In other cases they are perfectionists who don't want to do something unless they are confident that they can do it perfectly. Both are people who are afraid to make a mistake. They are afraid of failure.

These are also the same people who can pose challenges while you are trying to implement a performance coaching programme. They often don't respond well to goals that are challenging, preferring instead goals that fall into the realm of their current expertise and experience.

Another difficulty with these employees is that we often find ourselves doing things to try to avoid the inevitable hassles that always seem to happen when we delegate increased responsibilities to them. We either do the work ourselves or delegate the tasks to other members of the team, and in doing so we begin to overload everyone else.

The key difference between Mr Impossible and the Whiner is that Mr Impossible is not necessarily a negative person by nature. Such people are often proud of what they do and of their company and colleagues. They just aren't comfortable taking on more, new or different things. As a manager trying to get a job done, though, you will find that it doesn't take long for Mr Impossible to get on your nerves. This is where you have to be careful. Showing your frustration or impatience is not the way to deal with such employees.

Unlike with many other Employee from Hell types, it's best to stay away from positive encouragement with this type. They will probably perceive statements such as 'John, I know you can do this' as reflections of flaws in your management capabilities – either you don't understand the magnitude of what you are proposing or you are overestimating their capabilities. The best way to deal with these employees is to move as slowly as possible with them. Break the project or task in hand into many smaller components, and allow them to grow into the components gradually. The smaller the component, the smaller the consequences of failure. The smaller the consequences, the smaller the risk. The smaller the risk, the easier it becomes for the employees to accept the work. If the project isn't easily broken down, give them a little more time to complete the task so that they can make sure they will be successful.

If it is impossible to break things down or allocate more time, let them know that you are aware of how they feel but that you still expect them to do it. When they finally do successfully complete the project or task, remind them of their earlier misgivings, and then tell them that you knew all along they were able to do it.

Many management books will encourage you simply to reassure employees ahead of time that the job is easy and that they should have no problem getting it done. I've seen this approach fail far more often than I have seen it succeed. Why? When you think it through, the answer is obvious. They have already convinced themselves that the task won't be accomplished easily, and they have already voiced their opinion to you. Saying something like 'This job's an easy one, John. You could do it with your eyes closed' only sends the message that you don't value the employee's opinion and aren't prepared to listen.

That approach can also cause employees to create a self-fulfilling prophecy. As they stew over having to do the task despite having voiced their concerns, they can become much less focused and productive. The next thing you know, the task doesn't get done. They have, in essence, 'proved' to you that they were right in the first place. You'll be much further ahead with these employees if you acknowledge their opinions and then try to ensure that they are able to achieve their goals. Save your encouragement for after the fact, when you can tell them of your complete faith in their ability to accomplish the task.

## Social Butterfly

My company was doing some work with a large property development firm, and one of the women I met told me how she was constantly overwhelmed with work and that there just weren't enough hours in a day to do all the things she had to do. She wasn't unpleasant, or negative, or whining. Quite the contrary, in fact – she was a very pleasant and upbeat person who was just always under a lot of time pressure. Our discussion turned to more pleasant things, and half an hour later our conversation had covered family, children and friends.

Over the next few days, as I was in the workplace, I began to notice how rarely she actually sat at her desk. Much of the time she was in other people's offices or standing with colleagues in the corridor. The discussions she was having rarely seemed to be about business. One time she was having an animated chat with a colleague about the recent company golf tournament; another time she was recommending a restaurant to somebody. Yet another time she was in a corridor discussing her plans for the weekend.

Everybody liked her. She was bright-eyed, bubbly, personable and an excellent listener. But I suspect that her time challenges at work had far less to do with her workload than with her interoffice social activities. She was a Social Butterfly.

The challenges with Social Butterflies are obvious. Not only are they not as productive as they could or should be, but they also hinder everyone else's productivity as they do their thing. They don't do it on purpose, and most of them would be devastated to learn the negative effects of their behaviour on their

companies and colleagues. They just happen to be gregarious –
but unfocused – individuals.

You have to be very careful when dealing with Social
Butterflies. They are, by nature, quite sensitive and, if not
approached properly, can become entirely demotivated. You
want to change their behavioural patterns, but you want to do
so without losing their positive attitude. Again it's time for the
good stuff–bad stuff–good stuff format – this time with a bit of
a twist.

Begin by telling the Social Butterfly how much you appreciate his or her positive energy, and compliment the employee
on his or her ability to build positive relationships. Assuming
that you like the employee, tell him or her so. Let the employee
know that his or her positive attitude is a valuable asset to you
and the company. The next step is to tell the employee that you
would like him or her to work a little on productivity and time
management. Tell the employee your reasoning is that, if he or
she can combine tremendous interpersonal skills with better
time-management skills, he or she will become an even more
valuable asset to you.

Most Social Butterflies have a strong desire to please and will
jump at the chance to increase their value to you and the
company. Pick a time for the two of you to meet, and begin with
the following basic time-management exercise.

Ask the employee to record every action over the next week,
in one-minute increments. Tell the employee to make sure he or
she records everything – from toilet breaks to telephone use to
cigarette breaks. Ask the employee to be diligent as well as
honest. When outlining the instructions, make sure the
employee understands that there will be no negative consequences whatsoever – regardless of the findings. Let the
employee know that, even if you find out that he or she actually
works only 15 minutes a day, he or she won't get in any trouble.

Monitor the employee for the first couple of days, making
discreet notes about the times of day you see him or her visiting
or doing other social activities. After two days, casually ask if
you can take a look at the log. Make sure that it is an informal

and brief glance, and quickly check the log against your notes. If it is fairly accurate – if there aren't a lot of significant discrepancies – hand it back to the employee and say 'Great!' If you notice that the employee is omitting a sizeable proportion of the activities you've noted, call him or her into your office. Say something like this: 'Barbara, this is great. I need you to be a little more precise, though, with your record keeping. I made a few notes during the day, and I just wanted to see if the two coincided, and there are a few discrepancies. For example...' Make sure that the employee recognizes this is not a condemnation or an accusation.

At the end of the week, set aside half an hour with the employee to go over the log. Create ahead of time an informal spreadsheet with six or seven different categories to indicate the major time consumers. Included in them may be telephone time, discussions not related to a project or task, meetings, breaks and so on. The first thing you'll notice as you begin to analyse the log is that, over the course of the five days, the amount of time spent on actual work progressively increased. As the employee filled out and reviewed the log, he or she became more and more aware of unproductive time and tried to correct it throughout the week.

Next, calculate the averages in each of the categories, and set targets for the second week. For example, if the average telephone call was seven minutes long, set the target at five minutes. If the average meeting time was 20 minutes, set the target at 15 minutes. Help the employee to identify areas that are stealing time. Show the employee how, by trimming the time stealers, he or she can add a significant amount of time to the working week. I went through this exercise myself many years ago and managed easily to recapture three and a half hours a week simply by shortening each phone call a bit.

Ensure that you give the Social Butterfly a lot of positive reinforcement as performance improves – and you'll be amazed at how much improvement there will be. After the initial two-week period, while you won't need the employee to continue filling out time sheets, you still have to remain diligent. Like all of us, the employee is susceptible to falling into old habits and comfort zones. When you pass the employee in the halls and hear him or her having a personal discussion, just look, tap your watch with a smile and walk away.

## Not My Job

*Damn it, Jim, I'm a doctor, not a bricklayer!*
'Bones' McCoy, Star Trek

There's an old joke about two construction workers with shovels working at the side of the road. One man would dig a hole 2 or 3 feet deep and then move on. The other man would come along behind him and fill in each hole. While one was digging a new hole, the other was 10 feet behind him filling in the previous one.

Joe, watching this for an hour and a half from his petrol station across the road, finally couldn't take it any more and walked over to talk to them. 'OK, I give up. What's all this digging and refilling of holes about?'

The two men looked at each other blankly, and then one turned to Joe and said, 'Well, we work for the government, and we're just doing our job – that's all.'

The two men returned to their shovelling.

'But one of you is digging a hole, and the other is just filling it up again. You're not accomplishing anything. Aren't you wasting the taxpayers' money?'

'Look,' one of the men told Joe, leaning on his shovel, 'it's not our fault, OK? Normally, there's three of us – me, Jim and Dave. First I dig a hole, then Jim sticks a tree in it and finally Dave here puts the soil back. Jim got laid off yesterday, so now it's just me an' Dave.'

It's unfortunate, but there really are people like that. People who will do their job, only their job and nothing but their job – no matter what the impacts might be on those around them. Nurses talk about doctors who won't even change a dressing. Solicitors' clerks tell of solicitors who don't even know where the filing cabinets are. I remember a colleague of mine once refusing to hold the front door of the office open as movers were bringing in his new furniture.

Margo Warren, an event manager, tells about keynote speakers with egos so large that common courtesy when off the stage seems to elude them. Margo herself is quite the opposite, and won't hesitate to put aside her title of 'manager' and pitch in if another set of hands is required to set up an event. And Stan Udaskin, general manager of a car hire firm, readily turns out in the most miserable of weather to help his drivers shuffle cars around.

Not My Jobs are people who consider themselves above such things. 'I didn't spend seven years at university,' I once heard a recent MBA graduate say, 'to do my own photocopying.'

This unique Employee from Hell becomes particularly challenging when someone in a weak moment unwittingly promotes the employee to a position where he or she can annoy people on a larger scale instead of just one person at a time. There is no easy way that I know of to deal with Not My Job, but there is one way that works. Be blunt. Brutally blunt. Horribly, directly, brutally blunt. Invite the employee into your office for a meeting. Have prepared three things: a glass of water, an organizational chart and a bull's-eye target.

When the employee sits down, come straight to the point. Let the employee know that he or she is teamwork challenged and that your goal in life at the moment is to correct that. Here's how your opening might sound: 'Charlie, there seems to be a challenge with your willingness to be a team player. The impression seems to be that you see yourself as being somewhat above some of the tasks that have to be done around here. I would like to take you through an exercise on perspective.'

The employee may well deny that he or she has a superior attitude. If so, let the employee know that you are prepared to give him or her the benefit of the doubt but that you still want him or her to go through the exercises. Begin with the glass of water. Ask the employee to stick his or her finger in it and leave it there for a few moments.

While the employee's finger is in the water, explain to him or her that, for the purpose of this exercise, the water represents the workplace, and the finger represents the employee. Convey to him that, when people pitch in and function as a team, they become the water – fluid, flexible and accommodating. The organization as a whole becomes responsive to and ready for as much growth as its structure will allow. When someone is not a team player, that person becomes a solid, and the organization ceases to be as flexible and responsive. (I have to warn you, by the way, that, as the employee is sitting there trying to make eye contact with you while he or she has one finger dipped in the water, it is very difficult to keep a straight face.)

'The most important thing to recognize,' you continue, 'is how very much more important the team as a whole is than any of us as individuals are.' Then ask the employee to take his or her finger out of the glass. 'Now take a look at the hole you left.' Remain quiet while you maintain eye contact. Look for signs that the employee might be getting the point.

Right after this exercise, direct the employee's attention to the organizational chart. Ask the employee to find him- or herself and circle his or her name or position. Point out all of the lines that connect each position in the chart. 'What would happen,' you now ask, 'if all these lines were broken? What if all employees reported only to themselves and never had to communicate with others?' Hopefully, the employee will be able to recognize that, should this happen, the company would cease to function.

'When people concern themselves with their own needs only, to the exclusion of those around them [begin circling positions as you speak], they begin to interrupt the flow created by these lines. We become islands unto ourselves. Even though each of these areas has its own set of goals and responsibilities, they all have to be able to work together for everything to function.' Give the employee the chart and suggest he or she pins it up by his or her desk.

Finally, hand the employee the bull's-eye. Tell the employee that, if he or she can't begin to be a little more respectful of the rest of the team, it might be as well just to tape the bull's-eye to his or her back. Whether it's someone on the current team or someone on a future team, eventually the employee is going to become the target of somebody's wrath.

The approach isn't particularly pleasant, but it is effective in sending the message on the importance of teamwork and communicating your expectations of the employee as a team member. There is a good chance that you will never have this employee's complete agreement or understanding – his or her selfish behaviour, after all, has been nurtured for many years – but at least you can have the employee's compliance.

## Heart on Sleeve

I have a good friend, Janet, who has a colossal challenge trying to take a holiday. She is in a relatively high-pressure job, and her second in command simply can't take the stress when she is away. Janet inevitably receives at least one or two crisis phone calls during her holiday and upon her return finds herself spending half a day just trying to reassure her employee that everything is all right. According to Janet, this employee is highly competent and, although maybe not as proficient as Janet, she definitely has the skill sets and knowledge to get the job done. Intellectually, she has what it takes, but she is challenged emotionally when it comes to dealing with the stress.

Some people just seem to lack the ability to manage their emotional states at virtually any level. Their moods can change without notice, and you never know which of their personalities will show up for work on a given day. It takes very little to get them upset or worried, but once they've achieved one of those states it is extremely difficult to get them out of it.

With most Heart on Sleeve people, this isn't something that you can just sit down and have a conversation about. Their very sensitivity makes it a difficult topic to approach. It's also unlikely that you'll be successful in attempting to teach them how to manage their emotions better. The best strategy, I believe, is for you to learn how to manage their emotions better.

Most emotional behaviour is patterned and progressive. Our emotional states are set off by triggers, and those triggers can be literally anything. A loud noise, a ringing telephone, somebody shouting, a bill in the post – anything. We suddenly find ourselves feeling depressed, angry, upset, frustrated, over-whelmed, unsatisfied and so on. Once the emotion has been triggered, the emotional state builds and expands until it either reaches an end point or another emotional trigger overrides it.

It's important to recognize that these escalations in emotions follow a distinct and recurring pattern each time. Even though the specific events that trigger the emotions may differ, the same thought patterns emerge every time. Like popping in a CD, the same old song starts to play in our heads – and it plays particularly loudly for the Heart on Sleeve employee.

To change patterned behaviour, you have to develop strategies to interrupt the pattern. Interrupt it significantly enough and often enough, and the pattern ceases to exist. The first step is to learn how to identify Heart on Sleeve employees' triggers. What gets them going? Which common events seem to trigger their counter-productive behaviour? Make a list of these things so that you're prepared ahead of time to deal with them.

The second step is to interrupt their emotional patterns through a series of highly focused, short-term tasks. As soon as you see their emotional states begin to change, give them a five-minute task that will take all of their concentration to complete. Ask for a monthly sales summary broken down by client. Ask for a handwritten summary of each difficult customer they have had to deal with over the past two weeks. Ask for a rough count of a certain type of stock you have. The task itself is less important than the time-frame you give – five minutes, and make it urgent.

As soon as they have completed the task, give them another one. Again, make it easily attainable but something that will require significant focus for five minutes. What you'll discover, after you have done this two or three times, is that they have lost the emotional state that began to build. Although they won't be conscious of what you are doing, the events that used to trigger certain emotional patterns will eventually begin triggering a more work-related focus.

In following this process, you will literally have begun to reprogramme the way in which they respond to certain triggers. Rather like Pavlov's dog, only without the drooling. It won't work all the time, and it certainly won't change Heart on Sleeve's inherently emotional personality. But it will gradually reduce both the nature and the severity of the incidents that most significantly affect performance.

## Unfocused

There is one type of Employee from Hell for whom work is just a tremendous inconvenience. It gets in the way of all other activities during the day. A senior HR professional I know tells about an employee who went around to her colleagues and various managers to share her most recently learnt moves from a belly dancing class. Another ran a phone sex line during working hours. Commissioned sales reps are notorious for having little 'side projects' (sometimes full-time jobs) that eat up their time.

For some people, their job is simply not a priority. And it doesn't seem to matter how much coaching and motivating you throw at them – nothing works. But don't feel bad. It's a good bet that the same people are equally unfocused in every other aspect of their lives as well. It really wouldn't matter who their boss was – that's just the way they are. They often don't feel a tremendous attachment to the job or the company. They have an exceptionally short attention span, and they are almost exclusively focused on themselves. They are constantly in search of either mental or physical stimulation.

The Unfocused employee is not always salvageable, but it's never a bad idea to give it a shot. Some activities, of course, such as the employee running the phone sex line at work or the commissioned sales rep being a full-time employee of two companies, must be dealt with directly and finally. Fortunately, most cases aren't quite that severe.

Sit down with such employees and explain exactly what in their behaviour is creating challenges. As always, make sure that you have some specific examples to help make the point. Tell them that you need all of their attention on their work and the job at hand. Let them know that, while you are prepared to support them in getting their job done, you can't do it all yourself – they need to pull their weight.

It's really the only approach you can take. Some of these employees, no matter how well you say it to them, will simply be unable to understand what the big deal is. They will think of you as just overreacting to a minor incident. Unfortunately, these employees often become perfect candidates for being set free.

Most Unfocused employees, however, will make the effort to change their behaviour. In many cases, they are simply unaware of what they've been doing or don't realize the extent to which they've been doing it. Most will be mortified and embarrassed when you point out just how much of an effect their behaviour is having on productivity.

## Temporally Challenged

The meeting begins at 9 o'clock. Everyone is there but Paul, but no one is surprised – Paul is late for almost everything. He is one of those time-challenged people who drive everyone else around him mad.

People who are chronically late for things are everywhere, and their behaviour can range from being just a little annoying to being highly disruptive. A senior executive I once worked with used to be so chronically late with client meetings that our company literally began to lose business. (Needless to say, he's not there any more.)

To be honest, when I was younger, I was also chronically late. Not for important things such as business appointments or golf games, of course, but when it came to anything else I was always the one straggling in 15 minutes after everyone else. It wasn't until someone pointed out how selfish my behaviour really was that I began making an effort to change it.

Chronically late people have a dramatic and insidious impact on a company. The first and most obvious impact is the amount of other people's time that gets wasted. The biggest effect, however, is in the subtle (and usually unintentional) message they send. When someone is chronically late, that person sends the message that neither you nor the company is very important.

There are a couple of strategies that I've seen work for the Temporally Challenged. The first is to quantify the consequences of their actions for them. The next time a meeting is delayed because of someone's tardiness, have a meeting afterwards with the person and go through a little mathematical equation with him or her. You may have to do a little preparation, but your meeting might go something like this:

> Paul, there were six people in that meeting. If we pick an average salary of, say, £40,000 (use his salary as the example), that's £240,000 in annual salaries. That's £120 per hour, or £2 per minute. You were 10 minutes late today, and in doing this you've wasted £20 of the company's money. That might not seem like a lot to you, but you're late a lot. How often? Two, three times a week for different things? A hundred times a year? Now we're into thousands of pounds – just in employee costs. When you factor in the cost of lost productivity, it becomes many times that. The bottom line, Paul, is that I simply can't afford to have you being late to meetings any more.

Finish by asking for the employee's commitment, and make sure that you monitor the employee on a regular basis.

The second approach is equally direct but appeals more to the employee's sense of empathy for colleagues. Have a meeting with the employee, and point out the message the employee was sending to the others. Here is an example of how you might present it:

> Paul, being late for things every once in a while is acceptable. It happens to everyone. But it's happening with you more often than just once in a while. While you no doubt always have good reasons, I don't think you recognize the message that you are sending to everyone else. Being late for a meeting once sends the message 'Oops, I slipped up.'

> Being late on a number of occasions sends the message 'My needs are more important than everyone else's.' I am sure that that is not the impression you are meaning to give people.

As in the first example, finish by asking for the employee's commitment, and make sure that you monitor the employee on a regular basis.

## All about Me

A few people out there truly believe that the world and you owe them a living. At times bordering on a narcissistic personality disorder, these people feel a certain sense of entitlement. They have unreasonable expectations of special treatment and literally do not understand why they aren't the centre of everyone else's universe. They typically struggle with fundamental customer service principles because the concept of putting the needs of someone else first makes them uncomfortable. In meetings and workgroups, they translate everything into 'How does this affect me?'

All about Me is different from Not My Job in that All about Me's are not particularly conscious of their behaviour. They see themselves as discerning, particular, selective and hard to please, but they perceive those to be positives – reflections of character. They are rude and abrupt and at times seem almost to enjoy watching the people around them become uncomfortable. On the rare occasions that they express empathy – when it is expected of them – they make a big show of it so that everyone can see. All about Me's gain a feeling of power by being hard to please. They regularly send food back to restaurant kitchens. They burn through suppliers who don't treat them as though they are their only customer. They frustrate employees who don't display visible respect and adulation. Whenever I meet one, I think of a saying I once heard: 'Never give power to someone who can't live without it.'

All about Me's are particularly challenging Employees from Hell to deal with because, while they aren't particularly good team players, they rarely do anything wrong. Their response will typically be 'Yes, I have high standards – I'm not going to apologize for that.' What are you supposed to say to that? 'We don't want high standards around here?' The best way that I know to deal with All about Me's is on a situation-by-situation basis. Focus on the manner in which they say things instead of the actual things they are saying. Use questions to maintain control of the conversation. Be prepared, however; All about Me's can become very defensive.

Their first line of defence will be to question why you are even bringing the issue up in the first place, and they will express strong reluctance to recognize the need for change in their choice of language. They will try to dismiss any attempt you make by using deflecting questions and comments.

Let's say, for example, you're in a restaurant with one, and that person decides to return some food. Your conversation may go like this:

Charlie: Waiter, the chicken is dry, the rice is cold and the vegetables are anything but crispy. I was wondering if you would take this back and bring me something that is actually edible.
You: [After the waiter has gone.] Charlie, how might you have said that differently?
Charlie: What?
You: How might you have said that a little more pleasantly? How might you have phrased that so that the waiter would want to bring the food back instead of just feeling as though he had to bring it back?
Charlie: Why is that important?

It may sound like a flippant comment, but Charlie actually doesn't understand why it is important. Answers such as 'Being nice to people pays off' or 'You should try being nicer to other people' will have no effect on All about Me's because they simply don't think that way. Unless they see a direct and immediate pay-off to themselves, being nice to people is irrelevant.

The fastest way to have them change their behaviour is to let them know that you expect them to be nice. You expect them to be courteous, and you expect them to be considerate of other people's feelings. They will want to debate the point and ask you why, but don't explain. Simply tell them that it is what you expect and that it isn't negotiable. Your conversation at the restaurant now might finish like this:

> Charlie: [Deflecting.] Why is that important?
> You: It is important to me. I expect courtesy and awareness of other people's feelings in the workplace, and this is a good place to practise. So tell me, how might you have said that a little more pleasantly?
> Charlie: [Deflecting.] What's this all about?
> You: It's about courtesy and presenting things in a more positive manner, Charlie. It's very important to me, and I expect it of the people who work for me. It's an area that you need to work on. Now tell me, how might you have spoken to the waiter a little more pleasantly?
> Charlie: [Deflecting.] I don't understand. What has brought this on?
> You: Work with me, Charlie. Tell me how you might have presented that a little differently.

In the example, Charlie continues to deflect the request, hoping to draw you into a debate. The key is to avoid this debate and not to lose focus on your original request. Charlie will probably never really understand why he has to do it, but he will do it if you stick to your guns. The next step is to repeat this process each time you see him exhibit similar behaviour. It's a painful and arduous process, but he will eventually get the message.

## The Skunk

Every now and then you run into an employee who has some kind of persistent odour. It can be body odour, bad breath, smelly shoes or stale cigarette smoke. It makes everyone uncomfortable, yet, like a real skunk, the perpetrator never seems to notice.

The best way to deal with an odoriferous employee is the direct but gentle way. Your goal is to correct the problem while keeping embarrassment to the minimum. You want to present it to the employee as a friend, and you don't have to let on that anyone other than you notices the odour. Begin by acknowledging that it is an embarrassing subject. Let the employee know that you're mentioning it because you respect him or her. Be plain, and be brief. Don't stay around long after you break the news – doing so will just increase the embarrassment. Here is an example of how you might approach this problem:

> *You: Sam, there's something I want to talk to you about. It's kind of embarrassing, and I don't really know how to bring it up, but... well... I don't think you notice it, but you have a bit of a body odour problem. It's not really horrible, but it is noticeable. I'm really sorry to bring it up like this, but, well, I have a lot of respect for you, and I thought I should tell you before it becomes a problem for you.*

Choosing your words carefully is paramount. On the one hand, you don't want to play the problem down so much that the employee does nothing about it; on the other hand, you don't want to come right out and say something like 'You stink!' Be direct but gentle.

## Yeahbut

If I were ever to open an excuses shop, I would have no problem finding staff or stock. There are a great number of people out there who absolutely excel at excuses. 'Yeahbut it wasn't my fault.' 'Yeahbut I'm really busy.' 'Yeahbut it's going to take a lot of time.' 'Yeahbut that's not how it works.'

Yeahbut, yeahbut, yeahbut. One word with the power to turn the best of intentions into distant memories. From time to time, we hear it in our training sessions – typically in our customer service and sales programmes. 'Yeahbut,' the employee will tell us, 'this is [insert the name of any city on the planet here], and our customers are different.' It's getting harder to keep a straight face every day.

Once, while I was coaching in one of the shops of a large fashion retailer, two employees tried to convince me why they shouldn't proactively greet customers. They wanted no part of it. 'Yeahbut,' they told me vehemently, 'our customers are different from the customers in other shops...' As fortune would have it, at the very moment they were telling me this, three customers walked into the shop laden with bags from at least five other fashion retailers in the shopping centre. I couldn't resist. 'Yeahbut,' I said, 'what about them?'

The best way to deal with the chronic yeahbutter is continually to point out that behaviour and to encourage the person to reword his or her statements every time. Here are some examples.

## Call centre

*Supervisor: Jane, I'd like you to try to resolve more of these customer complaints without escalating them to a supervisor.*
*Jane: Yeahbut they ask for a supervisor; what am I supposed to do?*
*Supervisor: There's another one of those yeahbuts again! I think maybe what you meant to say was 'OK, do you have any suggestions as to what I can do that might work better?'*

## Sales

*Boss: Allan, I'd like you to increase your number of cold calls by 10 a week, all right?*
*Allan: Yeahbut I'm already doing 50. How am I going to do more prospecting and still keep up with my follow-ups?*
*Boss: Was that a yeahbut I heard? I think what you meant to say was 'Of course, boss, I'll give it a shot. It's going to be a challenge to do that and keep up with my follow-ups, but I'll certainly try.'*

**Figure 13.1** No yeahbuts

## Office

> *Boss: Sandy, it looks as though I'm going to need those reports on Thursday instead of Friday, as I originally thought.*
> *Sandy: Yeahbut I'm already in the middle of three other projects! I can't just drop everything.*
> *Boss: There's one of those yeahbuts again. Try this: 'OK, boss. I do have some other projects on the go – which ones should take priority?'*

Eventually, if you remain consistent, your employees will develop an awareness of their language pattern and gradually remove 'yeahbut' from their vocabulary.

## Liars, cheats and thieves

If there is ever a time when the decision to set an employee free is clear cut, it's when someone lies, cheats or steals. Don't think twice; don't hesitate; don't negotiate. Just dance the person out the door as fast as you can. Regardless of whether the victim was a colleague, the company, a customer, a supplier or you personally, the best solution for everyone is unceremoniously to cut the employee loose.

# Conclusion

Every now and then – when I'm walking through a shop, standing in an office or talking on the telephone – I meet someone who prompts a screaming thought: 'Who the hell hired this person? What was the employer thinking?' I hear the employee saying incredibly stupid things and see the employee behaving in inexplicable ways. I watch the employee bumbling, stumbling and mumbling while his or her colleagues and managers look on in embarrassment. I see customer service people with dead faces and deader voices. I witness shameless acts of selfishness and narcissism.

But, inevitably, no sooner do those thoughts flash through my mind than I begin to see different things. I see the secondary school student-turned-shop assistant who's never been asked to smile. I hear call centre employees who have never been told that they talk too quickly, too softly or too abruptly. I see senior managers who have never been taught the basics of managing people. I see employees trying to do a good job but not getting any support from those around them.

It's then I realize that, at one level or another, we all have the capacity to be Employees from Hell. And, as bosses, we have the influence to create even more Employees from Hell.

Perhaps the most important thing I've learnt is that Employees from Hell are really not very different from you or me. They are typically decent people who just do stupid things from time to time. The encouraging part is that, in most cases, we can do something about it. In *Dealing with the Employee from Hell*, I've tried to give you a few highlights of some of those things. The solutions aren't always pretty, but neither are they complicated – the important thing is that they work. And, even on those rare occasions that they don't work, I hope I was able to communicate the concept that your destiny and the destinies of those who report to you are largely still in your hands. Any action is better than no action, and doing nothing is rarely, if ever, an acceptable option.

Begin by examining your work environment. How might it be contributing to employee challenges, and what, if anything, can you do to correct it? Then take a look at yourself. What skill sets can you develop as a manager that will have a positive impact on the people around you? Follow this assessment with a close look at your Employees from Hell. Why are they behaving this way? What's behind their behaviour? Talk to them. Listen to them. Learn from them.

Yes, when the frustration really gets to you, and your Employees from Hell are just more annoyances among your workday pressures, it might seem as though the simplest solution is just to fire them and put an end to it. Sometimes, too, that is the best solution. But try not to make it your first or only alternative.

First, give them a chance. They may turn out well after all.

# Further reading
# from Kogan Page

*Accounting for Non-Accountants: A Manual for Managers and Students*, 6th edn, 2005, Graham Mott

*Be Positive*, 2000, Phil Clements

*Better Business Writing*, 2002, Timothy R V Foster

*Bids, Tenders and Proposals: Winning Business Through Best Practice*, 2nd edn, 2005, Harold Lewis

*Bridging the Culture Gap: A Practical Guide to International Business Communication*, 2004, Penny Carté and Chris Fox

*Business Etiquette*, 2nd edn, 2000, David Robinson

*The Business Plan Workbook*, 5th edn, 2005, Colin Barrow, Paul Barrow and Robert Brown

*Communicate to Win*, 2nd edn, 2005, Richard Denny

*Communication at Work*, 2001, Judith Taylor

*The Complete Mind Makeover: Transform Your Life by Changing the Way you Think*, 2005, Ros Taylor

*Creative Business Presentations: Inventive Ideas for Making an Instant Impact*, 2003, Eleri Sampson

*Cross-cultural Communication: The Essential Guide to International Management*, 2003, John Mattock

*Dealing with Difficult People*, 2001, Roy Lilley

*Develop Your Assertiveness*, 2nd edn, 2000, Sue Bishop

*Develop Your NLP Skills*, 2000, Andrew Bradbury

*Developing Your Staff*, 2001, Patrick Forsyth

*The Effective Leader*, 2003, Rupert Eales-White

*Empowering People*, 2nd edn, 2000, Jane Smith

*The First-Time Manager: The First Steps to a Brilliant Management Career*, 3rd edn, 2005, Michael J Morris

*A Guide to Working for Yourself*, revised 22nd edn, 2004, Godfrey Golzen and Jonathan Reuvid

*A Handbook of Management Techniques: The Best-selling Guide to Modern Management Methods*, 3rd edn, 2001, Michael Armstrong

*Hard-core Management: What You Won't Learn from the Business Gurus*, 2003, Jo Owen

*How I Made It: 40 Successful Entrepreneurs Reveal All*, 2004, Rachel Bridge

*How People Tick: A Guide to Difficult People and How to Handle Them*, 2005, Mike Leibling

*How to be an Even Better Manager: A Complete A to Z of Proven Techniques and Essential Skills*, 6th edn, 2004, Michael Armstrong

*How to Generate Great Ideas*, 2000, Barrie Hawkins

*How to Grow Leaders: The Seven Key Principles of Effective Leadership Development*, 2005, John Adair

*How to Manage Meetings*, 2002, Alan Barker

*How to Manage Organisational Change*, 2nd edn, 2000, D.E. Hussey

*How to Motivate People*, 2000, Patrick Forsyth

*How to Negotiate Effectively*, 2002, David Oliver

*How to Prepare a Business Plan*, revised 4th edn, 2004, Edward Blackwell

*How to Run a Successful Conference: Planning and Logistics, Keeping to Budget, Using Technology and Delivering a Winning Event*, 2nd edn, 2000, John G Fisher

*How to Write a Business Plan*, 2001, Brian Finch

*How to Write a Marketing Plan*, 2nd edn, 2000, John Westwood

*Improve Your Communication Skills*, 2000, Alan Barker

*The Inspirational Leader: How to Motivate, Encourage and Achieve Success*, 2005, John Adair

*Law for the Small Business: An Essential Guide to all the Legal and Financial Requirements*, 11th edn, 2004, Patricia Clayton

*Make That Call*, 2nd edn, 2000, Iain Maitland

*Making Innovation Happen*, 2001, Michael Morgan

*Marketing Plan Workbook*, 2005, John Westwood

*Motivate to Win*, 3rd edn, 2005, Richard Denny

*Not Bosses But Leaders: How to Lead the Way to Success*, 3rd edn, 2002, John Adair

*Powerful Reports and Proposals*, 2003, Patrick Forsyth

*Raising Finance: A Practical Guide for Business Start Up and Expansion*, 2004, Paul Barrow

*Selling to Win*, 3rd edn, 2006, Richard Denny

*Shut Up and Listen!: The Truth about how to Communicate at Work*, 2004, Theo Theobald and Cary Cooper, 2004

*Start Up and Run a Profitable Consulting Business*, 2nd edn, 2004, Douglas Gray

*Start Up and Run Your Own Business*, 3rd edn, Jonathan Reuvid and Roderick Millar, 2004

*Starting a Successful Business*, 5th edn, 2005, Michael Morris

*Stay Confident*, 2001, John Caunt

*The Strategic Planning Workbook*, 2002, Neville Lake

*Strategic Thinking: A Practical Approach to Strategy*, 2nd edn, 2000, Simon Wootton and Terry Horne, 2000

*Succeed for Yourself: Unlock your Potential for Achieving Success and Happiness*, 3rd edn, 2006, Richard Denny

*Successful Presentation Skills*, 2nd edn, 2000, Andrew Bradbury

*Successful Project Management: Apply Tried and Tested Techniques, Develop Effective PM Skills and Plan, Implement and Evaluate*, 2000, Trevor Young

*Successful Time Management*, 2003, Patrick Forsyth

*Taking Minutes of Meetings*, 2001, Joanna Gutmann

*Team Building*, 2000, Robert Maddux

*Ultimate Business Presentations Book*, 2003, Martin Yate and Peter Sander

*Using the Internet Smarter and Faster*, 2000, Brooke Broadbent

*Working Abroad: The Complete Guide to Overseas Employment*, 2nd edn, 2005, Jonathan Reuvid

*Write That Letter!*, 2nd edn, 2000, Iain Maitland

*Writing Effective E-mail*, 2000, Nancy Flynn and Tom Flynn

**Dealing with the BOSS FROM HELL**

A GUIDE TO LIFE IN THE TRENCHES

SHAUN BELDING

0 7494 4452 5  paperback  144 pages